DATE DUE			

JANE ADDAMS

Recent Titles in Greenwood Biographies

JANE ADDAMS

A Biography

Robin K. Berson

GREENWOOD BIOGRAPHIES

GREENWOOD PRESS
WESTPORT, CONNECTICUT · LONDON

Library of Congress Cataloging-in-Publication Data

Berson, Robin Kadison.
   Jane Addams : a biography / Robin K. Berson.
     p. cm. — (Greenwood biographies, ISSN 1540–4900)
   Includes bibliographical references (p.   ) and index.
   ISBN 0–313–32354–2
   1. Addams, Jane, 1860–1935. 2. Women social workers—United States—Biography.
3. Women social reformers—United States—Biography. I. Title. II. Series.
HV40.32.A33B47   2004
361.92—dc22   2004010978

British Library Cataloguing in Publication Data is available.

Library of Congress Catalog Card Number: 2004010978

ISBN: 0–313–32354–2
ISSN: 1540–4900

First published in 2004

Greenwood Press, 88 Post Road West, Westport, CT 06881
An imprint of Greenwood Publishing Group, Inc.
www.greenwood.com

Printed in the United States of America

The paper used in this book complies with the
Permanent Paper Standard issued by the National
Information Standards Organization (Z39.48–1984).

10 9 8 7 6 5 4 3 2 1

CONTENTS

Photo essay follows page 63.

SERIES FOREWORD

In response to high school and public library needs, Greenwood developed this distinguished series of full-length biographies specifically for student use. Prepared by field experts and professionals, these engaging biographies are tailored for high school students who need challenging yet accessible biographies. Ideal for secondary school assignments, the length, format and subject areas are designed to meet educators' requirements and students' interests.

Greenwood offers an extensive selection of biographies spanning all curriculum related subject areas including social studies, the sciences, literature and the arts, history and politics, as well as popular culture, covering public figures and famous personalities from all time periods and backgrounds, both historic and contemporary, who have made an impact on American and/or world culture. Greenwood biographies were chosen based on comprehensive feedback from librarians and educators. Consideration was given to both curriculum relevance and inherent interest. The result is an intriguing mix of the well known and the unexpected, the saints and sinners from long-ago history and contemporary pop culture. Readers will find a wide array of subject choices from fascinating crime figures like Al Capone to inspiring pioneers like Margaret Mead, from the greatest minds of our time like Stephen Hawking to the most amazing success stories of our day like J.K. Rowling.

While the emphasis is on fact, not glorification, the books are meant to be fun to read. Each volume provides in-depth information about the subject's life from birth through childhood, the teen years, and adulthood. A thorough account relates family background and education, traces personal and professional influences, and explores struggles, accomplishments, and contributions. A timeline highlights the most significant life events against a historical perspective. Bibliographies supplement the reference value of each volume.

INTRODUCTION

Who was Jane Addams? At times in her life, the founder of Hull-House (one of the United States' earliest settlement houses), social reform author, and Nobel Prize winner was the most honored, recognized, and revered woman in America; at other times she was called the most dangerous, wicked, conspiratorial figure in the country, the evil spider at the center of a vast, nefarious web of un-American, anti-Christian scoundrels. She experienced youthful optimism, crippling self-doubt and despair, moments of insight and moments of obliviousness. She had many successes and major, heart-breaking failures. Her struggles, her hopes, her courage, vision—even her limitations—speak directly to us as we too work at constructing lives of worth and meaning.

Addams lived from 1860 until 1935. In many ways she embodies the experience of the middle-class Victorian woman in a period of enormous change—a period of both possibility and restriction, transition and virulent resistance to that transition. She was a child of small-town, almost rural frontier America—an environment of tremendous ethnic and religious homogeneity; yet she found meaning and direction to her life in founding Hull-House in the most vividly, raucously diverse immigrant urban neighborhood she could find, where her neighbors were impoverished, quite literally alien, and overwhelmingly Catholic or even Jewish. She was frequently described in the most cloying religious terms as a saint, a martyr, an icon of self-sacrifice; yet she denied all that and never embraced any sense of conventional religiosity. She saw her chosen path as one of great richness and self-fulfillment and rejected any hint of self-sacrifice. She argued strenuously for women's suffrage without any deep sense of feminism: her demand for the vote was not based on any concept of equal rights or philosophical justice, but on the very Victorian image of women as somehow more morally sensitive and alert than men. She had no training in sociology or social work, but she became a prolific, widely read, and deeply influential sociologist. She was seen as a quintessentially American figure until she basically renounced nationalism in favor of a broadly humane internationalism. She was a profoundly private, reserved woman whose very public life was in some ways minutely observed and documented.

The range of Addams's concerns, of her active social and political involvement, is astonishing. What follows is only a partial list of the organizations to which Addams belonged, many of which she helped to found:

> National Council of Women
> National American Woman Suffrage Association
> Friends Equal Rights Association
> College Equal Rights Association
> National Association for the Advancement of Colored People
> American Civil Liberties Union
> World Peace Foundation
> American Peace Society
> Woman's International League for Peace and Freedom
> Association for International Conciliation
> Women's Christian Temperance Union
> Daughters of the American Revolution
> National Congress of Mothers
> Association of College Alumnae (later the Association of American
>   University Women)
> American Federation of Labor
> National Women's Trade Union League
> Carnegie Endowment for International Peace
> International Kindergarten Association
> National Federation of Settlements (she was the first president)
> National Conference of Charities (she was the first woman president)
> Young Women's Christian Association
> Women's National Committee of the Socialist Party
> Peace Committee of the International Council of Women
> Southern Federation of College Women

Addams campaigned for the abolition of child labor and of the death penalty, for factory safety laws, for a range of worker protections and rights, for women's suffrage, immigrant rights, freedom of speech, court reform, prison reform, temperance, disarmament, and civil rights—among others. She was never content simply to denounce a vice or antisocial practice; she worked to study, as objectively as possible, the origins of the situation—to understand the weaknesses and motivations of all the players and to offer effective alternatives. Almost every item of social or economic reform from 1895 to 1930 grew from research she had initiated, protests she had helped organize, testimony she had given or encouraged; her commitments included labor and housing standards, the eight-hour workday, old-age and unemployment insurance, political campaign reform, public playgrounds, and juvenile justice.

Addams was careful to couch her reform programs in the language of tradition and nineteenth-century, middle-class values. She didn't so much defy conventional roles as she redefined them to suit her purposes, all the while claiming not to. She made the language of proper femininity, domesticity, and piety serve her in startlingly new contexts, but she never called herself a radical or an iconoclast. (Her enemies were more than willing to call her those things and much worse.) She draped her goals in older costumes: assumptions of womanliness as nurturance, of Christian (Protestant) piety as a motivation—even while she changed the functional definition rather than the term itself. Her costume was so altered by her own personal needs and responses, by her enormous social conscience and vision, that the costume eventually became a disguise. We may well ask to what extent she was aware of this sleight of hand and whether in some ways she needed to believe in her own disguise as well; as with so many questions we ask of the dead, we may find no reliable answers.

All Addams's kaleidoscope involvements were grounded in an image of the universal human family, of a broad embrace of inclusiveness that built from the individual and particular into a sweeping sense of cumulative goodness and justice. In her autobiography, *Twenty Years at Hull-House*, she spoke of "broadened sympathies toward the individual man or woman who crosses our path; one item added to another is the only method by which to build up a conception lofty enough to be of use in the world" (Addams [1910] 1990, p. 58). Because her vision always summoned a particular caring response to a specific situation, she was wary of dogma and labels.

Addams was a magnificently stubborn, determined woman. As a student at Rockford [Illinois] Female Seminary, she resisted considerable pressures to become a missionary; whatever respect and admiration she might voice for missionaries, she did not accept the role for herself. She did not believe that any specific revealed doctrine offered the only path to the moral life. She called her ethics Christian, which may well have been a necessary gesture to ensure the support of wealthy benefactors. But she insisted that she was not referring to any contemporaneous denomination, that she believed rather in "the original primitive communal and completely tolerant, self-sacrificing and self-effacing kind" of Christianity (Levine 1964, 30).

Jane Addams believed that real democracy involved *social* democracy, the enactment of shared human awareness in the details of daily, grubby existence. She believed that the value of any idea lay in the quality of action that it inspired; in this she was very much in the tradition of American pragmatism, and her philosophy shared much with the great American philosophers John Dewey and William James. At times she called herself "conservative," by which she meant that she wanted to conserve and protect the precious and vulnerable: to Addams, this entailed fighting for protective legislation for working women and children, as well as establishing a museum at Hull-House especially to honor and preserve immigrants' old-world crafts and skills.

Addams's great underlying goal was human unity. To her, there were multiple stages on the path toward true justice and cooperation. The first involved charity, the recognition and alleviation of immediate suffering. The second, upon which all her hopes rested (and sometimes foundered), involved education, the awakening of the moral conscience. The third, which she believed would be the natural outgrowth of the second, called for governmental commitment to reform in the processes of society.

Was Addams a radical? She demanded an activist welfare state, a recognition of communal goals and responsibilities on a scale unheard-of at the time. But she did not want to acknowledge the reality and depth of class conflict, and while her understanding of human growth and environment seems basically socialist, she tried not to accept any ideological labels. Perhaps faith in conscience and cooperation *was* her ideology. The threads that wove Jane Addams's life were strong and remarkably consistent: idealism, service, ambition, openness, a willingness to search, skepticism, a passionate need for self-respect. These threads may have got tangled and frayed at points in her life, but they almost always ran recognizably and reliably from her youth. In 1919, while discussing famine relief in Europe after the First World War, she commented, "After all, what is human life but a working forward together, with our human needs and spiritual needs so intertwined that it is impossible to separate one from another?" (*Report* 1920, 195).

TIMELINE OF EVENTS IN THE LIFE OF JANE ADDAMS

6 September 1860	Jane Addams born in Cedarville, Illinois.
1863	Sarah Weber Addams, Jane's mother, dies.
1868	John Addams, father, marries Anna Haldeman.
1877	Enters Rockford Female Seminary.
1881	Graduates from Rockford.
1881	John Addams dies.
1882	Undergoes back surgery performed by stepbrother Harry Haldeman.
1883–85	Travels in Europe.
1887–88	Second trip to Europe.
September 1888	Opens Hull-House with Ellen Gates Starr.
1895	Appointed garbage inspector of 19th Ward.
1896	Travels to England and Russia; meets novelist Leo Tolstoy.
1898	Joins Anti-Imperialist League.
1905–9	Serves on Chicago School Board.
1907	Serves as delegate to first National Peace Congress.
1909	Signs Niagara Call; helps found National Association for the Advancement of Colored People.
1912	Serves as delegate to Progressive Party national convention; seconds nomination of Theodore Roosevelt for president.
1915	Attends first meeting of future Women's International League for Peace and Freedom (WILPF), The Hague.

1917   Maintains pacifist position after U.S. entry into First
               World War.
1919   Presides over second women's peace congress, Zurich;
               brings food relief to Germany and Austria; con-
               demned by Lusk Committee of New York State Leg-
               islature; helps found American Civil Liberties
               Union.
1921   Presides at third WILPF congress, Vienna.
1923   Travels around the world.
1924   Presides at fourth WILPF congress, Washington,
               D.C.
1926   Presides at fifth WILPF congress, Dublin.
1929   Presides at sixth WILPF congress, Prague; resigns as
               president of WILPF.
1931   Awarded Nobel Peace Prize.
21 May 1935   Dies in Chicago; buried in Cedarville.

ABBREVIATIONS

EGSP   Ellen Gates Starr Papers
JAMSS   Jane Addams Manuscripts
JAPM   Jane Addams Papers on Microfilm
SCPC   Swarthmore College Peace Collection
WILPFP Women's International League for Peace and Freedom Papers
WPPP   Woman's Peace Party Papers

Chapter 1

BEGINNINGS

In American mythology, the frontier has always beckoned to eager, ambitious young men. Cedarville, Illinois, was a frontier village in 1844 when 22-year-old John Huy Addams arrived, and he was hard-working and ambitious enough to meet any definition of the pioneer spirit of the times. Fifty years later, his daughter Jane would find and love that same pioneering spirit in the impoverished immigrants of her crowded Chicago slum neighborhood. Her need to recapture the driving animus of her father's life is indicative of the utterly central role his image played in her own life.

John Addams and his new bride, Sarah, were both from old Pennsylvania families; John Addams's ancestors had been granted land by William Penn in the seventeenth century. John and Sarah found Cedarville, 14 miles south of the Illinois-Wisconsin border, a welcoming home where they prospered. Addams, a successful miller, rose quickly to prominence within the community. When they first came to Cedarville, John and Sarah lived in a tiny two-room house with a loft; 10 years later John Addams built a large, two-story home of gray brick, the biggest house in Cedarville. He was first elected to the State Senate as a Whig in 1854; one of the founders of the state's Republican Party the following year, he would serve in the senate for six more terms. Addams was deeply committed to community development, frequently making loans to neighbors for various improvements. His civic activism and political involvement were inspirations for his youngest daughter.

Sarah Addams gave birth to nine children, only four of whom lived to adulthood. Three infants died before their first birthdays, and one child died at the age of two.

Jane, the eighth child, was born on September 6, 1860. Sarah, five years older than her husband, was a paradigm of helpful, self-sacrificing, community-minded, frontier womanhood, known throughout the town for her generosity and compassion. In January 1863, 46 years old and pregnant herself with her ninth child, she went to assist at the birth of another woman's baby—a difficult, exhausting delivery, as it turned out. When Sarah finally got home, she collapsed in premature labor, produced a stillborn son, and died a week later. Jane was not yet two and a half years old.

When Sarah died there were five children in the family: Mary, who at 17 functioned as Jane's mother; 13-year-old Martha; James Weber, the only surviving son, who was 10; Alice, who was 9; and Jane, the youngest living child. The entire family was devastated by Sarah's loss. Weber, the only son, was a shy child who may well have felt intimidated by his powerful father; after Sarah's death he retreated into a deep depression that would leave him in fragile mental health for the rest of his life. Mary and Alice took over the responsibility of caring for the others; both women would enter into unhappy marriages to demanding, insensitive men. Martha would die of typhoid at the age of 16, while a student at Rockford Female Seminary. Of all the children, only Jane would grow up to struggle successfully against the claims of overwhelming family duty.

Until her father remarried when Jane was eight, Mary took most of the responsibility for raising her, and she managed to provide a basically secure, affectionate household; the bond between Jane and Mary was especially deep and lifelong. Mary saw tremendous strength of character in her little sister; after a trying visit to the dentist when Jane was 11, Mary wrote to Alice, "She is brave…she is a dear good child…a comfort not only to Pa but to Ma [Anna, the stepmother]. She is *true* as she can be; if she makes a promise, she will keep it" (Diliberto 1999, 53). In 1871 Mary married John Linn, Cedarville's Presbyterian minister. Jane remained devoted to Mary and to her large, troubled family.

Jane, known as Jennie, had comfort, safety, privilege, companions, and easy access to the beauties of local nature. Frontier society was still largely open and democratic, although there is no question that John Addams's position in his community provided extra layers of protection and delight for the child. Clearly, Jennie recognized that hers was the largest home in town, but she attended the one-room schoolhouse with the children of farmers, mill workers, and other laborers, and these children were her friends. What set her apart from her classmates was the high-minded inspiration of her father and his role in guiding her early reading. While strict goals and behavioral expectations were set for her, her rural childhood laid the foundation for her profound belief in the basic goodness and redeemability of human nature. Throughout her life, Jane would treasure the memory of this relatively fluid society, and she would come to see rigid class distinctions as inimical to social and ethical growth.

John Addams was the single most important influence on Jane. She adored him, she worshipped him, she was desperate to earn his approval, she strove to emulate him. She wanted so much to be like him that she wished her hands looked like his, with their scars from carving millstones and their thumbs flattened by years of rubbing flour between his fingers. Addams was an early friend of Abraham Lincoln and a committed abolitionist. He was stern, remote, and righteous. Surprisingly, this small-town entrepreneur on the edge of the frontier in the middle of America had strongly international interests. He was passionate about political freedom throughout the world: he followed the career of the Italian revolutionary Giuseppe Mazzini, and he mourned deeply when Mazzini died.

Addams's unwavering support of such international figures, his abolitionism, and his firm belief in women's suffrage all set standards of human mutuality and responsibility that Jane absorbed eagerly. He guided her reading, going so far as to bribe her: five cents for each of Plutarch's *Lives* that she read, and a quarter for each volume of Washington Irving's *Life of Washington*. She was a serious child, small, fragile, and frequently ill, suffering from a slight curvature of the spine that would trouble her into adulthood. She described herself as an ugly duckling, pigeon-toed and graceless. She worried that she was a disappointment and embarrassment to her tall, imposing father. She was burdened with an active, demanding conscience and strained by her constant efforts to merit her father's approval; childhood photos offer us a face of sad introspection that seems older than its years. She was somewhat spoiled, willful, and extremely stubborn. One childhood playmate commented years later on her determination, "If she began doing it, you couldn't make her quit" (Linn [1935] 2000, 28).

In 1868 John Addams married Anna Haldeman, a widow with two sons. (Two other sons had died in infancy.) If Sarah Addams had typified the early ideal of the frontier life, Anna Haldeman Addams represented the next stage of socialization: she was desperate to be perceived as cultured, *civilized*, and proper; she considered herself aristocratic and intellectual, although she ridiculed women's rights advocates and could not imagine any higher aspiration for a proper young woman than motherhood. The new family dynamics were complex and strained. Anna's elder son, Harry, later married Jane's older sister Alice; he was a brilliant, troubled alcoholic, the surgeon who would operate on Jane's back in 1885. The younger son, George, was a few months younger than Jane. From the time they were 8 until Jane went to college at 17, Jane and George were inseparable companions who encouraged each other's intellectual and social growth. It was Anna's intention that Jane and George marry, but Jane turned down his proposal. (Anna probably never forgave her.)

There was a great deal of tension and mutual misunderstanding between the two women as Jane grew. Anna believed that Mary had spoiled Jane and indulged a degree of invalidism; Anna was far stricter and less sympathetic to the child. Jane resented Anna's treatment bitterly, but she never rebelled. Anna Haldeman Addams brought her piano and a love of the arts into her second marriage. Under Anna's hand, Jane took drawing lessons and studied the piano in the larger town of Freeport, six miles away. In some ways Anna's influence was positive; she provided an easy attitude toward wealth and culture that would allow Jane to be at ease later in circles of privilege and power. Nonetheless, as she grew Jane felt stifled and oppressed by Anna's social expectations, and Anna could neither understand nor accept the choices that Jane made: despite her considerable wealth, Anna never contributed any funds whatsoever to the upkeep of Hull-House.

John Huy Addams was a towering presence in the public life of his community as well as in his daughter's life and imagination. He was a religious man with a profound distrust of specific dogmas and denominations: he contributed annually and equally to each of Cedarville's four churches—Methodist, Lutheran, Evangelical, and Presbyterian—but he never joined any of them, and he never had Jane baptized. When the child once asked him what he "was," he replied that he was a Quaker, although not birthright—that is, born into the religion. Certainly he believed in broad tolerance, inclusivity, and a deep sense of civic responsibility. But his professed Quaker leanings never asserted themselves as pacifism; he supported the Civil War and voted for every military bill that came up during his tenure in the state senate. In later years Jane would attribute her pacifism to her father's influence, as she did so many other worthy goals and characteristics, but the documentary evidence does not support her belief.

As a teenager, Jane was not happy with her physical appearance. She considered her nose to be a lump of flesh utterly lacking in character and cursed with eight "horrible" freckles; she was disappointed in her straight hair and tried to curl it on a set of rollers made for her by the village tinsmith. At 16, she was an awkward child who couldn't dance; her spinal curve and pigeon toes increased her feeling of gracelessness. She had reluctantly learned the required needle crafts, and John Addams had demanded that all his daughters learn to bake good bread, but Jane disliked domestic tasks and would far rather have been walking in the woods, gathering plant and mineral specimens, or reading.

Jane was fascinated by social reform. She read the novels of Charles Dickens and ached for the suffering of the poor; she read Ralph Waldo Emerson and determined to become an active, responsible citizen. She read the great figures of Victorian literature: Matthew Arnold, George Eliot, Thomas Carlyle, Herbert Spencer, John Stuart Mill, Leo Tolstoy, even Karl Marx. Jane was thrilled by the writing of Scottish historian Thomas Carlyle, especially his 1841 *On Heroes, Hero-Worship, and the Heroic in History*. Imbued by her father with a relentless conscience and sense of purpose, Jane responded to Carlyle's deeply conservative notion of the "great men" of history, who led the unthinking masses in the path of righteousness and duty; how ironic that in her adult life Addams would utterly reject this theory of leadership and place her greatest faith in the common people's wisdom, innate goodness, and capacity to learn. In July 1876, while visiting Philadelphia with her family, Jane had a chart of her head done by a phrenologist. (Phrenology, the "science" of reading a subject's character from the topography of the skull, was taken very seriously in mid-nineteenth-century America.) With an eerie foresight, the phrenologist reported of Jane, "Mental powers greater than physical...strong will and inclined to be very obstinate.... Moral faculties very much larger than religious. Inclined to be skeptical...she would never be a proselyte, not sectarian, thinks everyone has the right to believe what they please...large imagination, but under good control, if she builds castles in the air she always has some good foundation for them" (JAMSS).

Chapter 2

THE ROAD TO HULL-HOUSE

At the age of 16 Jane was all of five feet, three inches tall, and she weighed just 95 pounds. She was considered pretty, with dark, searching eyes, but she was as vulnerable to social awkwardness and self-doubts as any adolescent. She was full of ideas, hopes, and unfocused ambition. She wanted desperately to go to Smith College in Northampton, Massachusetts—one of a few recently opened women's colleges that offered an academically rigorous and stimulating environment. Jane had traveled to Smith in January 1877, where she had taken and passed the entrance examination. But John Addams, a trustee of Rockford Female Seminary, was unwilling to let his daughter go so far away. He insisted that she attend Rockford, nearby, where both Mary and Alice had gone; with great disappointment and reluctance, Jane complied.

There was considerable controversy over any higher education for women. The most fundamental conflict was over the nature and proper role of *Woman*. In 1873, Dr. Edward H. Clarke, a professor at Harvard Medical School, published the influential *Sex in Education*. He argued that higher education damaged the reproductive systems of women and led to "nervous prostration"; too much stimulation to the brain drew blood from the uterus and could cause that racially vital organ to atrophy. The intelligence and educability of women have been denigrated by men throughout most of history; in the last quarter of the nineteenth century such doubts were heightened by a deeply racist, nativist response to the surge of immigration from southern and eastern Europe: American political, social, and religious leaders argued that authentic American culture—which was of course white, Protestant, and middle-class—was

endangered by the dark-skinned, largely Catholic and even Jewish immigrants. The only patriotic response for white, native-born, Protestant
women was to save their race by having white, native-born, Protestant
babies; it was their duty to stay healthy (and stay home) and stem the tide.
Anything that could be claimed to jeopardize that mission was seen as
perverse and disloyal.

Nonetheless, some men could recognize limited functions for a limited
education for women. Rockford Female Seminary had been chartered in
the 1840s by the Presbyterian and Congregational churches. Its head-
mistress, Anna Peck Sill, arrived in 1849, fired with the goal of educating
good Christian women. Although it did not grant degrees until 1882,
Rockford was known as the "Mount Holyoke of the West." Its stated goal
was to produce "Christian Mothers and Missionaries for the Evangeliza-
tion of the World" (Phillips 1974, 50). The curriculum was heavily
grounded in the classics, in languages, history, mathematics and natural
sciences, and in ethics (called *moral science*). The perspective was utterly
Protestant: there was never room for doubt where discussions in ethics
classes might lead. There was enormous pressure on the girls to step into
the role of Christian missionary and/or wife.

Jane Addams would be neither. Throughout her years at Rockford, Addams resisted the pressure—"I was singularly unresponsive to all these
forms of emotional appeal" (Addams [1910] 1990, 31). In fact, she
claimed later that learning to stand up to this kind of zealous demand had
actually trained her to be independent. She respected but did not like
Anna Sill; in a private journal at the time, she commented, "She [Sill]
does everything from love of God *alone,* and I do not like that" (JAMSS).
While many of the young women at Rockford did become missionaries,
medical assistants, teachers of the blind, or librarians in stark frontier
towns, Addams was at this point much more certain of what she didn't
want to do than of what might give her a sense of purpose and direction.

Eager, a little skeptical, and brave, Addams threw herself into life at
Rockford, determined to learn as much as she could. This was her first experience of a wider circle beyond Cedarville, her first opportunity to form
relationships with many other curious young women and to develop loyalty to them. She seems to have been well liked and able to attract a wide
range of other girls to her dormitory room, but she was somewhat aloof
and formal. All the girls were addressed as "Miss" in their classes, but Addams preferred to be called "Miss Addams" out of the classroom as well.
For the rest of her life, even her closest associates at Hull-House would
recognize her reserve and refer to her formally.

Life at Rockford was disciplined, controlled, and rigorous. The quarters were Spartan, the meals sparse and deliberately unappealing, the dress austere and utilitarian. (Despite the required drab dresses, most young women wore tight corsets to cinch in their waists; Addams, disdainful of fashion, refused to wear a corset.) The day started at five A.M., when the girls had to empty the ashes and tend the stoves in their rooms—their only source of heat. The academic curriculum always rested on a foundation of proper womanhood and domestic competence. The students were expected to spend a minimum of one hour each day at domestic chores. Each student had to keep an account book and submit it for inspection once each month. The girls were required to keep a notebook in which they copied the long list of regulations, and they had to report their own transgressions each week. Irregular behavior could result in the imposition of demerits, which in extreme cases could lead to expulsion.

Despite Rockford's stated mission and rigid official attitude, many intelligent, determined young women from Illinois and Wisconsin flocked to the school. Addams was a vital, engaging young woman, part of a small circle of intense, intellectually demanding friends. Like so many other ambitious Victorian girls, Addams found a comfort and strength in her female friendships that she could not imagine in any relationship with a man. "I am a great admirer of Platonic love, or rather pure, sacred friendship," she wrote to a friend in 1877. "I think it is so much higher than what is generally implied in the word love" (JAPM). Addams and her friends set a rigorous cultural reading program for themselves, including the evolutionary theories of Charles Darwin, the art critic John Ruskin, Edward Gibbon on Roman history, and the notorious Thomas de Quincey's report of his drug taking adventures. One morning in their rooms they tried to capture his alleged transcendent insights by taking opium. (Opium, the basis of the popular sedative laudanum, was available fairly easily.) They did not achieve enlightenment; rather, they became sick and disoriented; a teacher found them, removed both the opium and the de Quincey, and lectured them severely.

Addams kept notebooks while at Rockford, in which she reported candidly on her feelings, observations, hopes, and fears. These journals reveal a young woman full of ambition and a strong if unfocused sense of destiny, as well as a profound if reluctant skepticism. "Solitude is essential to the life of man," she wrote. "All men come into this world alone and all leave it alone." Acknowledging her deep sense of personal moral responsibility, she noted, "Nothing is more certain than that improvement in human affairs is wholly the work of uncontented characters." And later, foreshadowing her own torment after graduation, she commented, "Our doubts are traitors and make us lose the good we often might win, by fearing to attempt" (JAMSS).

From her childhood rambles in a rural setting throughout her life, Addams had a strong interest in the sciences. Both her stepbrothers were deeply involved in science, Harry as a medical student in Germany and later physician, George at a more amateur level. At Rockford, Addams helped start a scientific society during her freshman year. The summer of her sophomore year, she studied comparative anatomy independently with George; in her senior year, she told George that she'd like to spend the next summer studying mineralogical chemistry.

Despite Addams's attractions to science, her first love was always literature and writing. She was elected president of the Rockford Literary Society, became a frequent and competent debater, and wrote numerous articles for the *Rockford Seminary Magazine*. As a junior, Addams was on the editorial staff of the magazine, where she was responsible for exchanges with publications from other colleges. She became the editor in chief her senior year. She was part of a rebellious group who wanted to make the magazine less pious and more involved with student concerns; even at this point, Addams functioned as a negotiator, trying to mediate between the student group and a disapproving school administration.

Perhaps the most important thing Addams took from Rockford was her friendship with Ellen Gates Starr. A deeply spiritual, artistic girl, Starr entered Rockford in Addams's class but stayed only one year. Addams was drawn strongly to Starr, admired her, and after she left Rockford, wrote to her constantly. They discussed issues of religion and faith—their struggle for it, their doubts about it, at great length—sometimes their letters rambled for twenty pages or more. Addams's letters to Starr display a fairly steady insistence on searching for the practical, applied impact of religion; she wondered how to develop one's highest, best attributes in the service of a larger good.

As in so much else of her life, Addams felt a driving need to understand her own feelings and to justify any position she took by its practical application; without having the vocabulary to describe herself, she was already falling into the leading American philosophy school of pragmatism. In her third year at Rockford Addams conducted a deliberate experiment on herself: for three months she did no praying whatsoever. The worst thing about it, she reported to Starr, was that she felt just fine. "I do not think we are put into the world to be religious," she wrote to Starr in the fall of 1879, "we have a certain work to do, and to do that is the main thing."

Starr was deeply tormented by her own issues of faith, and she urged her friend to get back to praying, but Addams was more comfortable looking for the hands-on implications of goodness. "You long for a beautiful faith, an experience," she wrote to Starr. "I only feel that I need religion in a practical sense, that if I could fix myself with my relations to God and the universe, and so be in perfect harmony with nature and deity, I could use my faculties and energy so much better and could do almost anything." She was more interested in Jesus as a moral figure than as deity. Again she wrote, "I can work myself into a great admiration for his life, and occasionally I can catch something of his philosophy, but he don't [sic] bring me nearer to deity....I feel a little as I do when I hear very fine music— that I am incapable of understanding.... but my creed is ever *be sincere and don't fuss*" (EGSP). Throughout her life Addams would resist formal, doctrinaire religion. Shortly before her death she confided to her nephew and biographer, "I never professed Christianity at Rockford, not til [sic] I was 25. If my father had lived I might never have joined a church at all, I suppose, but of course it is all very far back" (Linn [1935] 2000, 411).

Addams had been brought up with the image of her dead mother as a saintly figure of service and usefulness; her father seemed to combine high ethical principle with an energetic activist engagement in the world. Tangled as young Jane Addams was in the drapery of Victorian domestic piety, she longed to emulate both her parents. She often spoke and wrote in the Rockford student magazine about women's intelligence, moral sense, and right to be educated, as well as the responsibilities that education would bring. Throughout college she struggled to break beyond the rigid societal images of acceptable womanhood; of endless submissiveness, passivity, and domesticity; of being permitted to live only a surrogate half-life through one's husband and children. She often felt frustrated by all the restrictions; as she wrote to Starr, "Sometimes when I think of being hemmed in by these four walls I grow perfectly restless, but when I think what a good quiet place it is for study I become quite contented again" (EGSP). She accepted the ideology of women's higher moral qualities, but she insisted that these very qualities obligated women to move beyond the shelter of home and family and to apply their abilities in a wider world. In her junior year Addams organized an exhibition and festival focused on the image of women as bread givers in the Anglo-Saxon meaning, *hlaf dige*, the origin of the word "lady". Addams gave the major oration of the event, entitled "Bread Givers," in which she articulated the conventional notion that women's central role was one of service while also claiming a much broader perspective on service itself: "So we have planned to be 'Bread-givers' throughout our lives; believing that in labor alone is happiness, and that the only true and honorable life is one filled with good works and honest toil" (*Jane Addams* 1960, 104). The inter-twined image of bread as profound nurturance and woman as the generous custodian of life would run consistently throughout Addams's writing for the rest of her life. The address she gave as valedictorian of her senior class, entitled "Cassandra," offered the story of the mythical Greek prophetess Cassandra as a metaphor for the tragedy of all women: to be right and to be disregarded.

Addams was a member of the class of 1881 at Rockford, the first class offered the option of a real bachelor's degree. (This required extra course-work, which Addams had already done.) At first she declined the degree from Rockford, since she still had hopes of going to Smith College as orig-inally planned and receiving a B.A. there; a year later, she did indeed ac-cept her degree from Rockford. She was a loyal and generous alumna throughout her life. In 1886 she made the largest single gift ever made to the school by a Rockford graduate—$1,000 toward the purchase of sci-ence books. The following year Rockford made her a trustee, the youngest in its history. From 1891 until 1901 she held Hull-House summer schools on the Rockford campus, and in 1930 she endowed a professorship of so-cial science there. She spoke at numerous commencements.

After graduation from Rockford, Addams went home to Cedarville to rest and prepare herself for her journey east to Smith that fall. Instead, she suffered from a flare-up of her childhood back problems, from repeated colds, headaches, and general malaise. It was as though her immune sys-tem had collapsed, although she had had no real health problems while in college. Many historians have attributed her sudden decline to her fa-ther's death that summer, but the truth is that she abandoned her plans to attend Smith in July 1881, a full month before his unexpected death. It is true that neither her father nor her stepmother wanted her to go to Smith. Did they pressure her that summer? Was her undiagnosed illness a re-sponse? Family drama had long since cast her as the delicate, sickly daugh-ter—under so much pressure, did she accept that role again, did she step into invalidism to avoid having to assert her own rights over her parents' demands? Whatever the complex causality, she was launched into eight years of confusion, pain, and despair.

In August Addams accompanied her parents on a trip to northern Wis-consin. Near Green Bay, with no warning, her father was stricken ill, probably with a ruptured appendix, and died the next day. Understand-ably, Addams was shattered. Three days after his death, she wrote to Starr,

"The greatest sorrow that can ever come to me has passed, and I hope it is only a question of time until I get my moral purposes straightened" (Linn [1935] 2000, 66). Starr responded, "[Y]ou are too much like your father, I think, for your 'moral purpose' to be permanently shaken by anything, even the greatest sorrow" (EGSP). She struggled to find any meaning in life. Addams's beloved older sister Mary wrote to her, "You need not think that because he is gone, your incentive has perished.... He did not desire you to live for him but for the world, for humanity, for yourself & for Christ" (Addams 1965, 16).

But what did it mean, in practical, daily terms, to live for the world, for humanity, for oneself, for Christ? Were those goals even compatible? At a very basic level, the question really was: What are women capable of? What is their true nature? What is the purpose of their existence, under either divine or natural law? And of course, once that proper role is established, how can men keep women in their place? The controversies that swirled around the woman question tangled both race and class. It was ironic that women were being portrayed as weak and incompetent just as they were entering the workforce in ever greater numbers—and because higher education was denied them and so many professions were closed to them, most women who worked outside their homes did so in the hardest jobs, with no protection, no rights, long hours, and even lower wages than men got. Even the new, struggling trade unions barred women from their ranks. In the 1880 census over 2,500,000 women were listed as employed—roughly 15 percent of the workforce. Ten years later that figure had swelled to over 4,000,000 among whom were 300,000 girls under the age of 15.

To the late Victorians, class and race were virtually interchangeable templates. Poor, working-class women were not the same sort of creature as upper- and middle-class women; weakness, debility, timidity were taken as signs of good breeding. The last quarter of the nineteenth century also saw the rapid rise of the eugenics movement, which tried to base such racist theories on scientific principles of animal breeding. Proper women of the superior race (white Protestant, that is) were expected to be delicate, sensitive, and prone to illness. They needed protection and shelter if they were to produce the healthy babies the race needed from them.

Jane Addams certainly qualified for membership in that exclusive club of exemplary white women. She inherited substantial properties from her father and a sizable portfolio of stocks and bonds, worth roughly 60,000 dollars—a respectable sum at that time. Her private, independent income made it possible for her to have choices that were simply not available to most women. She did not need to work. She was an unmarried young woman with older siblings and many nieces and nephews. Tradition could expect her to move in with one of her sisters and devote herself to their lives and children.

Addams resisted the pull of tradition, but she had at this point no positive sense of direction for her life. Only a month after her father's death, Addams and her stepmother moved to Philadelphia, where Jane enrolled in the Woman's Medical College of Pennsylvania; she had decided to become a doctor during her senior year at Rockford. The Woman's Medical College, opened in 1850, was the first medical school to accept women. After the Civil War several more such women's medical schools opened, and women were accepted at three previously male university medical schools: Michigan, Cornell, and Johns Hopkins. The practice of medicine was attractive to many late Victorian women: it offered the sense of being of service to other women, and it provided a close-knit sisterhood with other women physicians and scientists. Medical school did not suit Addams, though, and she suffered increasingly from the spinal problems that had haunted her childhood. Addams dropped out of school after only seven months. She felt an overwhelming sense of failure, a despairing purposelessness, a debilitating passivity.

Addams was a textbook case of neurasthenia, the vague, generalized, and widespread malaise that afflicted thousands of women in the 1870s and 1880s. Women who were beginning to recognize broader possibilities in life, who could sense somehow that their own energy and intelligence might be useful and productive in society, felt increasingly stifled by the rigid restrictions and limitations of middle- and upper-class Victorian expectations. When the frustration and confusion of these women caused stress-related symptoms, their physicians claimed a pathological condition, the only cure for which was a retreat from over-stimulation—from any stimulation at all. Women of the "other" sort, who were laboring 12 and 14 hours a day under brutal conditions, seemed not to be as susceptible to neurasthenia as their more privileged sisters.

College women seemed especially prone to neurasthenia, which alarmed doctors and politicians alike. Many reports and studies during the period claimed to reveal much higher rates of illness and even insanity among educated women. Between 1800 and 1900 the birthrate among white Americans dropped by 50 percent, and it was true that college-educated women were far less likely to marry than their uneducated sisters. One study found that while 80 percent of women in general married, only 28 percent of college women did so. Fully 75 percent of the women awarded Ph.D.s by American universities between 1877 and 1924 never married. Of the 977 women in the 1902 *Who's Who*, almost one-half were unmarried (Diliberto 1999, 60). At the same time, immigration was rising, and many immigrants, whether Catholic or Orthodox Jews, produced large families. Clearly, higher education for women endangered the racial balance and health of the nation. By 1903 President Theodore Roosevelt could accuse white upper-class women of approaching "race suicide": "If Americans of the old stock lead lives of celibate selfishness...disaster awaits the nation" (Ehrenreich and English 1978, 135).

In February 1882 Addams entered the Hospital of Orthopedic and Diseases in Philadelphia, run by S. Weir Mitchell. Mitchell was the physician who "cared" for novelist Edith Wharton as well as Charlotte Perkins Gilman, author of "The Yellow Wallpaper." This searing novella chronicles Gilman's hideous experiences with Mitchell. Gilman was a 25-year-old writer and artist struggling to juggle marriage, work, and a demanding baby when she went to Dr. Mitchell. He advised her to go home and live an utterly conventional, unquestioning life of domesticity and obedience: "Lie down an hour after each meal. Have but two hours intellectual life a day. And never touch pen, brush, or pencil as long as you live" (Ehrenreich and English 1978, 102). Gilman went almost completely mad under this regimen before she rebelled and saved herself.

Addams spent six weeks in Mitchell's private hospital, enduring his rest cure with growing impatience. Her greatest fear was the sense of uselessness, of having no arena in which to offer something meaningful of herself. In April, still lost and dissatisfied, she returned to Cedarville with Anna Addams and tried to step into the maiden aunt role awaiting her in the family drama. Ten years later, she articulated clearly what the attempt had cost her: "The girl loses something vital out of her life which she is entitled to. She is restricted and unhappy; her elders, meanwhile, are unconscious of the situation, and we have all the elements of a tragedy" (Addams 1965, 38).

That summer, while she attempted to play the dutiful unmarried sister and deflected the romantic attentions of her stepbrother George, Addams still planned to travel east and enter Smith College. But her back pains grew steadily worse, and the fall found her undergoing complicated back surgery in an attempt to strengthen her spine. The surgery was performed by her older stepbrother, Harry Haldeman, who had married her sister Alice. In a frightening, painful procedure, he injected a caustic irritant into her back on either side of her spine; the expectation was that the resultant scar tissue would support the spine. For six months afterward, she was bedridden at the home of her older sister; for months after that, she wore a leather, steel, and whalebone brace. The enforced idleness and helplessness made her feel more lost than ever. In the spring of 1883 her older brother Weber suffered a complete mental collapse, stranding his wife and children. Jane Addams was the only family member available to pick up the pieces. She went to court to have Weber declared insane, arranged his commitment to a mental hospital, and assumed all the burdens of dealing with his distraught family and managing the extensive business properties he had inherited from their father (in addition to her own).

Handling these responsibilities well offered Addams a renewed sense of energy, competence, and good health. In July 1883 she sailed with her stepmother for a tour of Europe that would last more than two years. The party included Mary Ellwood, a Rockford classmate, Mary's sister Harriet, and their aunt. Despite a hectic schedule and the rigors of travel, her health improved steadily; she soon abandoned the detested body brace and never wore it again.

Addams kept a detailed log of her experiences, drinking in sights and details of art, culture, and local peoples as they traveled from Ireland to Scotland and England and on through the Continent. She chronicled vividly the towering cathedrals and museums as well as the sight of poor people, burdened workers, and hungry children, but her observations at this point were still distanced and conventional; only in retrospect, in her autobiography written 25 years later, did she give these moments the significance and weight of foreshadowing her later commitment. Her letters to family and friends reveal a developing sense of self-awareness, a recognition of the entire experience as somehow imposed and artificial. "I have constantly lost confidence in myself," she wrote to Ellen Starr in June 1884, "and have gained nothing and improved in nothing.... I have been idle for two years just because I had not enough vitality to be anything else" (EGSP).

Jane and Anna Addams returned from Europe in the summer of 1885; they had cut their trip short when they learned of Mary Linn's rapidly declining health. Anna had probably enjoyed herself on the trip more than Jane, and she was reluctant to sink back into the limited, small-town life of Cedarville. She also had an unmarried 25-year-old stepdaughter whom she was determined to launch into society—for both their sakes. Anna and Jane relocated to Baltimore, where Anna's son George was in graduate school and where Anna hoped Jane would find an acceptable social role as well as a husband (preferably George). Jane found neither. She du-

tifully dressed up, attended lectures, teas, and parties, tried to act the polite, decorous lady. She was utterly miserable. That fall, very much as a
traditional lady bountiful, she visited several local charities, including a
shelter for destitute children and an orphanage for African American
children where the education was industrial—that is, preparing the black
children to be good servants. It is an indication of Addams's immature vision at that point that she wholeheartedly approved of the venture.

These two years in Baltimore were probably the low point of Addams's
long, floundering struggle to find a purpose for her life. She felt lost, use-
less, meaningless. "I am filled with shame that with all my apparent leisure
I do nothing at all. I have had the strangest experience since I have been
in Baltimore, I have found my faculties, memory, receptive faculties and
all, perfectly inaccessible, locked up away from me" (EGSP). The summer
of 1886 found her back in Cedarville, faced with varied and enormous
family demands: her sister Mary Linn was pregnant again, and her husband was unhappy and difficult; stepbrother Harry Haldeman was drinking heavily and deeply in debt; brother Weber was in a psychiatric
hospital; and George Haldeman, the stepbrother who had wanted to
marry her, was sinking into a paranoid reclusive half-life. Unquestionably,
these people needed help; undeniably, Jane was conditioned to see response to need as one dimension of woman's usefulness—but she also recognized that her own needs had to be part of any such equation.

After another desperately polite season in Baltimore, Addams returned
to Cedarville and for the first time in her life took a job: teaching French
and German as a substitute at Rockford. She lasted one day on the job and
quit. She moved into her sister Mary's house to help with the growing
family, gave away her medical textbooks, and vowed never to try teaching
again. She was 27 years old, with no sense of purpose, confidence, or accomplishment. She had traveled widely, studied a great deal, submitted
several articles to magazines and had them all rejected. On the other
hand, she had learned to manage competently her inheritance from her
father, which provided a very comfortable income of $3,000 per year, and
the constant activity of dealing with a house full of children had strengthened her often precarious health. She decided to go to Europe again.

Addams took her second trip to Europe as a maturing woman learning
how to assume control of her life. She traveled with Ellen Starr and with
her beloved Rockford teacher, Sarah Anderson; recognizing the vastly different economic realities of their lives, Addams offered to pay half the
other women's expenses. This second experience of Europe was profoundly different for Addams. She handled logistics and arrangements,

she traveled alone on several occasions and stayed alone in strange cities. At one point she suffered a painful attack of sciatica and the doctor who treated her called her an invalid; she responded firmly that she was tough and strong, and she recovered quickly. In London Addams attended a meeting of match girls who were on strike, and she met daily with leading labor reform thinkers. Her social conscience, her recognition of her own responsibility to involve herself, was blossoming rapidly; the pieces of the puzzle were beginning to come together, although Addams herself later thought she had been slow to put them together.

In the spring of 1888 Addams and her friends attended a bullfight in Madrid. She would later describe the experience as searing and transformative: she was swept up in the ritualized, beautiful brutality and appalled by her own fascination. Her friends left in disgust, but Jane stayed on through the killing of five bulls. In *Twenty Years at Hull-House* she stated that this moment forced her to face the sterility of her constant search for more culture, more experience; it signified to her the core limitation of a life grounded only in esthetics; the bullfight was the ultimate extrapolation of a selfish pursuit of beauty and culture. It demonstrated to her in unforgettable ways that beauty was not an adequate goal for a person determined to be *useful*. She was done, she recalled, with the paralyzing sense of endlessly *preparing* for action rather than *acting*.

The very next day, in her memory, she told Ellen Starr of her childhood dream to have "a big house right in the middle of horrid little houses" (Linn [1935] 2000, 88). Starr responded with enthusiasm to the idea, and in discussions real possibilities began to take shape as the young women returned to London late that spring. As is often the case, Addams's 25-year-old memories, and the stylistic demands of popular American autobiography, rendered the moment rather more dramatic and decisive than it probably was. The plan developed gradually and seemed in significant part to depend on a chance encounter with one of the most intriguing, adventurous institutions of Victorian London: Toynbee Hall.

Toynbee Hall was a somewhat revolutionary social experiment in Whitechapel, a desperately poor district of London. It was started in 1884 by several young Oxford graduates trying to confront the multiple miseries of industrial London's poor, while at the same time providing themselves with an opportunity for the rigorous moral growth so favored in Victorian intellectual life. In the spirit of *noblesse oblige*, the wealthy young men of Toynbee Hall offered a variety classes and other services to the poor; what was novel was the notion that the middle- and upper-class men could learn as well from their experiences among the poor. Unmarried young men with jobs elsewhere were invited to become residents, to live at Toynbee Hall and involve themselves in the life of the community. Implicit in this is the recognition that there was indeed a community, that the poor had social structures and organization, that beyond the profound gulfs between the classes was the potential of shared humanity and even friendship. If the place tried to hang balanced between conservative and radical ideas about poverty and class, if it carried built-in contradictions, it was still braver and more humane than any conventional approaches to urban injustice and inequality.

In June 1888 Jane Addams traveled from London to Canterbury to see the great cathedral there. Taking tea in Canterbury, she met a friend of the Reverend Samuel Barnett, Toynbee Hall's first head resident and guiding spirit. The friend, hearing of Addams's growing interest in active reform, offered her a letter of introduction to Barnett (without which, in Victorian society, she would have been unable to approach him); on their return to London, Addams and Sarah Anderson visited Barnett at Toynbee Hall. Addams was captivated. She wrote eagerly to her sister Alice, "It is so free from 'professional doing good,' so unaffectedly sincere and so productive of good results in its classes and libraries so that it seems perfectly ideal" (Davis 1973, 49). She was determined, she wrote later, that "I should at least know something at first hand and have the solace of daily activity" (Addams 1965, 28). She was done with the everlasting "snare of preparation." She saw in Toynbee Hall a wonderful precedent through which American college women, "smothered and sickened with advantages" (Linn [1935] 2000, 87), could make meaningful use of their abundant and undervalued energies and knowledge. She had found a focus, a path through the wilderness of despair and boredom. The path would lead to "a big house right in the middle of horrid little houses": Hull-House, a rambling, ramshackle, decrepit old mansion stranded in one of the most crowded, desperate slums of Chicago.

Chapter 3

HULL-HOUSE AND HOPE

When Jane Addams and her dear friend Ellen Starr returned from Europe in the summer of 1888, they had already determined that their big house, their Toynbee-like experiment in the mutuality of life, would be located in Chicago. Heading to their vastly different homes and families, they agreed to meet in Chicago right after New Year's Day of 1889. What was the city like that had become the locus of their new dream?

In 1889 Chicago was a city of almost 1,000,000 people, expanding rapidly into the outlying small towns; by 1890 there were an additional 200,000 Chicagoans, making the population only 400,000 fewer than New York City's. Almost three-quarters of that population were foreign born. By far the largest ethnic group was German, with 400,000 residents. There were over 200,000 Irish, 54,000 "Bohemians [Czech]," and 20,000 Italians. In these decades before the Great Migration of African Americans from the South, the black population of Chicago was relatively small—barely 15,000. There were thousands of Russians, Poles, and Jews of all sorts.

The city throbbed with the energy, power, and ruthlessness of money. It was the home of the world's first real skyscraper, the ten-story Home Life Insurance Company Building, completed in 1885. It had just built the Auditorium, the largest opera house in the United States, and would soon complete the tallest office building in America. The Newberry Library, which would become a world-famous focus of scholarship in the humanities, would open soon. The University of Chicago, largely funded by John D. Rockefeller, was under design. In 1893 the city would host the Chicago Exposition, a massive extravaganza in celebration of Columbus's 1492 voyage to the New World—an occasion that gloried in the wonders of technology, progress, and the American Way of Life.

All the glitter and energy and self-congratulation rested uneasily on the straining backs of an exhausted and poorly treated labor force. A skilled laborer might expect to earn $2.50 to $4.00 after a 10-to-12-hour day. Unskilled workers might make $9.00 to $12.00 for a 12-hour, 6-day week. Small children hunched over piecework in sweltering or freezing sweatshops might earn 4¢ per hour.

There was among wealthy Chicagoans a deep distrust and fear of the poor, an image of them as less than fully human, in need of stringent control. The city still reeled with memories of the infamous Haymarket Riot in 1886: During a mass protest meeting of striking workers demanding an eight-hour day, a bomb had gone off, killing several policemen. The actual culprit was never found, but the strike's organizers, most of whom were not even at the rally, were held responsible. Of the eight men tried and convicted, all but one were immigrant radicals—anarchists whose beliefs and hopes for working people appalled the men in power. The lone American-born anarchist among them, Albert Parsons, was an ex-Confederate soldier who had been run out of Texas for marrying a half-Mexican woman who had been a slave—the power structure of Chicago could more easily forgive the former than the latter. The atmosphere in town was deeply tainted by popular theories of eugenics, of class superiority, and of indifference if not hostility to the immigrant poor.

Into this environment, in January 1889, stepped Jane Addams and Ellen Starr. They were animated, full of hope, convinced that they could make real improvements in the lives of the poor while imbuing their own lives with meaning. Addams read everything she could on social reform movements, and corresponded with fledgling settlements in New York City; she had even studied bookkeeping while in Cedarville, so that she could feel more competent and confident handling their business affairs. They took rooms in a respectable boarding house and set about finding the right neighborhood for their center—their settlement—and the right sponsors to make it all possible.

Legend frequently labels Hull-House the first settlement in America, but—as with much of legend—this is not true. Toynbee Hall in London had inspired other reform-minded young Americans as well. One of them was Stanton Coit, a graduate of Amherst College who was in graduate school in Berlin when he visited Toynbee in 1885. On his return to New York City the following year, Coit founded the Neighborhood Guild (later called University Settlement), vaguely modeled on Toynbee, the first settlement in America. Both Toynbee Hall and the Neighborhood Guild accepted only male residents. A group of vibrant, compassionate young college alumnae, among them Jane Robbins, M.D., Vida Scudder, Jean Fine, and Helen Rand—were also deeply moved by Toynbee Hall; they were determined to provide similar challenges and opportunities for college women. Their College Settlement Association organized the college women of New York—among them a youthful Eleanor Roosevelt—to support and engage in settlement work; under their guidance, the Rivington Street Settlement on the Lower East Side opened a week before Addams and Starr moved into Hull-House.

Through the next quarter-century, even as immigration, uncontrolled industrialization, and economic crisis widened the wealth disparities and exacerbated the struggles of the urban poor, the settlement movement washed like a refreshing tide across the country. In 1891 there were six settlements in the United States. By 1897 there were 74, and at the turn of the century there were at least 100. Early commentators tended to ignore the efforts of black and rural communities; the first African American settlement was Locust Street Social Settlement in Hampton, Virginia, founded in 1890 by Hampton Institute graduate Janie Porter Barrett. Within a year, there were at least three black settlements in New York and Chicago.

Traditional perspective cast poverty as inevitable, immutable, almost racially grounded; the poor were seen as shiftless, worthless, the degenerate agents of their own suffering. Late nineteenth-century reform attitudes represented a profound shift toward seeing poverty as a *result*, a condition with causes in the environment and in economic and social policies—a condition, therefore, that could be altered by changes in that environment and those policies. (This conservative/liberal split has been somewhat glibly summarized as the nature versus nurture debate.) An optimism grounded in that belief sustained many settlement workers through early difficulties, roadblocks, and defeats.

The activists in the settlement movement saw themselves as distinct from earlier traditions of Christian charity, which frequently dispensed largesse even while it held the impoverished individual somehow morally responsible for his failures; it tried to hold the poor to strict character and behavioral standards that many of the charitable could not or would not meet. The settlements may have drawn from the best of compassionate religious tradition, but they refused to proselytize; not even the Reverend Barnett, the first director of Toynbee Hall, would tie his programs tightly with the strings of religion. It is true that the vast majority of settlement workers came from and reflected middle- and upper-class Protestant social expectations, but for the most part they rejected religion as their overriding motivation. When the National Federation of Settlements was founded in 1911 (with Jane Addams as its first president), it did not accept as a member any settlement founded with a religious mission.

In the depth of an inhospitable Chicago winter, Addams and Starr began their search for the right neighborhood, the right house, the right benefactors. They visited several churches with active missions; they looked into nonsectarian missions as well. They spoke at churches, at club meetings, at private gatherings, and they impressed people with their vision and dedication. Ironically, given her history of resisting any evangelical role, Addams seemed to be inspired by a kind of missionary zeal for this new venture. "There's a power in me," she wrote to her sister Alice, "a will to dominate which I must exercise, they hurt me else" (JAPM).

Addams recognized the religious component of much of their support. She had never been and would never be a conventionally religious person, but she knew that many of her potential backers were exactly that. Ever a pragmatist, she used the vocabulary of piety to elicit support for her plans, much as she would employ the vocabulary of Victorian womanhood and social niceties while determinedly dragging those terms into a new landscape of direct meaning. Addams had finally been baptized in the Presbyterian church in Cedarville in the fall of 1888; she saw the gesture as one born of confusion, an attempt to put an end to her questions rather than a positive choice. In personal correspondence she revealed that she felt no excitement or commitment, that the church did not provide the sense of belonging and community she so desperately wanted. She joined the church formally in September, 1889, only three weeks before she and Starr moved into Hull-House. It can be argued that Addams joined a church, at least in part, because she knew she would need the mainstream respectability and acceptance such membership conferred.

The vision the two young women offered their audiences was one of shared, transcendent human experience. Addams insisted always that the real growth and learning would occur first in the settlement residents, who would be invigorated in an environment of service and activity. "She has worked this out," Starr reported to a friend, "of her own experience and ill health" (EGSP). At teas, luncheons, and receptions, Addams and Starr struck a deeply resonant chord with many upper-class young men and women. The women especially could identify with the terrible paradox of the educated women with no venue for her energy; alumnae of Smith, Vassar, and Wellesley all came to speak with them after such gatherings. The extent of response from wealthy young people convinced Addams and Starr that they could build an independent support base and maintain their project free of any (implicitly male) institutional oversight.

At one meeting, Addams and Starr met an enthusiastic young architect, Allen B. Pond, who offered to show them around the city's seamier neighborhoods. Addams was drawn to Italian communities, but Starr pushed for someplace where French or German was spoken, and logically, they could more easily expect that their college-educated residents would know French and German. They finally agreed on the infamous 19th Ward, and they noticed a suitable house in the district, but for several months couldn't find it again. In May they finally rediscovered the house at 335 South Halstead Street, just off Polk Street.

South Halstead Street ran for 32 miles through the entire city of Chicago. Polk Street crossed it at midpoint, between the stockyards to the south and the shipyards on the north branch of the Chicago River. The area between the two was the 19th Ward, one of the most crowded, poverty-stricken, problematic immigrant districts in the city. It was home to 19 different nationalities—about 50,000 people, most of whom, for reasons of gender, citizenship, or misinformation, could not vote. Housing was appalling—mostly rotten wooden structures that had once been single-family homes but were hideously crowded by 1890. There were no fire escapes, no indoor plumbing, no systematic removal of garbage or waste from the many stables. There were not enough schoolroom places for the children in the ward, but then, so many of the children were at work and unable to attend school in any event. Unregulated factories and sweatshops dominated the neighborhood; frightened immigrants hunched over piecework shirts, dresses, and hats in poorly lit, unventilated basement shops. There were 255 saloons in the ward, eight of them in the immediate neighborhood of Hull-House; that worked out to one saloon for every 28 voters. There were seven churches as well, only three of which conducted services in English. Addams described the neighborhood in an early address: "The streets are inexpressibly dirty, the number of schools inadequate, sanitary legislation unenforced, the street lighting bad, the paving miserable and altogether lacking in the alleys and smaller streets, and the stables foul beyond description" (Addams [1910] 1990, 59).

The house that would become internationally known as Hull-House was a large, elegant brick structure set well back from the street, with high ceilings, large rooms, and still-intact moldings and other architectural details. It had been built as a suburban residence for Charles Hull, a wealthy

Chicago businessman, in 1856, when Chicago had only 85,000 residents. Originally, the house stood among open fields and towering oaks, but the rapidly expanding city piled up around the house, and Hull moved on. In the 1870s the house was rented to a Catholic mission, and later several small shops and a tenement flat occupied the second story. By the time Hull died in 1889, half the building was a saloon, while a furniture factory and shabby rental rooms filled the rest. The new owner, Hull's cousin Helen Culver, was among those impressed by Jane Addams, and she was glad to provide space for the new settlement. Within a year, Culver was so convinced of the project's value that she turned the house over to Addams, with its land and with other lots she owned on the block, Culver's early generosity made the future of Hull-House possible.

In an atmosphere of heady anticipation, Addams and Starr furnished Hull-House with an eclectic mixture of old family furniture and new items they delighted in discovering in Chicago shops. They both envisioned this as their permanent residence; they brought family heirlooms, books, dining room silver. They were determined to provide an environment that was elegant and gracious—and they were, after all, expecting to house other well-bred young women like themselves, who would pay for their room and board and contribute their own assorted abilities to the enterprise. At this early stage, Addams and Starr stressed their venture's similarities to Toynbee Hall, in a kind of public relations campaign to emphasize the respectability of the settlement. They recognized realistically that it was far more problematic for society to contemplate the notion of unmarried young women living on their own in a noisome neighborhood populated by dark-skinned immigrants; it was essential to reassure prospective residents and their families with an outstandingly upper-class atmosphere. There was no notion here of sacrifice or of Spartan conditions to be endured; quite the contrary: they were convinced that Hull-House should stand as a beacon of culture, and serenity in that hectic, harried neighborhood. As Addams recalled, "Perhaps no young matron ever placed her own things in her own house with more pleasure than we did" (Addams [1910] 1990, 57). On September 18, 1889, the two women moved in with a housekeeper, Mary Keyser.

Once again, Addams's vocabulary is significant. Neither Addams nor Starr was likely ever to marry; they both saw Hull-House as their own home and hoped that the incoming residents would become their family—an ideal family of choice, of shared ideals and commitment. From its inception Hull-House was designed to meet the needs of both residents and neighbors. There was a sense of reciprocity, an awareness that the residents would get as much as they would give, an appreciation of much that was valuable in the alien cultures of the neighborhood. James Linn, Addams's favorite nephew, was almost her age and spent a great deal of time at Hull-House. As he recalled in his biography of her, "Jane Addams went to Hull-House to live, no more to help than to be helped; no more to provide opportunities for others, than to provide herself with an opportunity; no more to satisfy the longings of others than to satisfy her own longings; no more to 'save' than to be saved" (Linn [1935] 2000, 106).

As in so much else in her life, Addams refused to impose anything on others. Her faith in the ethical power of education was almost limitless; she believed that, offered a clear range of options, human beings were capable of making informed, morally responsible choices. Her understanding of culture and beauty was certainly grounded in her own education and environment: she was to some extent an unabashed esthetic elitist. The graceful furniture, the conventionally beautiful paintings and engravings that decorated Hull-House, were intended to offer visiting locals a sense of the possible, a range of goals and aspirations that their own crowded, filthy tenements could not. But her ideals of growth were inclusive rather than exclusive; that is, she hoped that their uneducated immigrant neighbors would learn to enrich, not replace, their own cultures with the great art, literature, and music of the "Western canon."

The family Addams and Starr drew to them was truly spectacular. The women who gathered at Hull-House those first few years embodied an energy, intelligence, determination, and sheer courage that is awe inspiring. Addams and Starr were soon joined by Julia Lathrop, Florence Kelley, Alice Hamilton, and Mary Rozet Smith. For the next 45 years, despite divergent careers and geographic distance, these women created for each other the loving embrace of a family. Without the demands of husbands or children, they were able to support and respect each other with an intensity almost impossible to find in the Victorian world outside Hull-House. The secure base of warmth and understanding allowed them to focus their remarkable energy on wider commitments.

Ellen Starr was not from a wealthy family; she was forced to leave Rockford Female Seminary after only one year. She became a teacher of English and art history, blending her intense spirituality with an almost mystical aesthetic. In Chicago she taught at the Kirkland School, a fashionable school for the privileged that nonetheless maintained a rigorous curriculum. Starr's position at Kirkland made her the contact through whom many wealthy young women were first exposed to Hull-House; her role in the experiment's early days was critical. At first, Starr applied her

passionate nature to social issues as well as to art. She was a fierce advocate of trade unions and would even join picket lines. James Linn commented, "[S]he crusaded down dirty streets, and frail and gentle as she was
in appearance, was no more daunted by policemen than she would have
been by Saracens or dragons" (Linn [1935] 2000, 131). In 1895, after
studying bookbinding in England, Starr set up a bindery at Hull-House;
she devoted herself to its operation and largely withdrew from the public
programs of the settlement.

Julia Lathrop came to Hull-House along paths similar to Addams's. Her
father was a wealthy lawyer and politician in Rockford; her mother, a
member of Rockford's first graduating class, was a sophisticated suffragist.
Like John Huy Addams, Lathrop's father was an abolitionist and an early
associate of Abraham Lincoln; like John Addams, he fostered in his
daughter a sense of her responsibility to act ethically as well as the sense
that she could find a way to do so. Lathrop entered Rockford Female Seminary in 1876, but after only one year was able to do what Addams had
hoped to: she transferred to Vassar College, a demanding, secular institution in New York. Lathrop studied law after graduation, went home to
Rockford, and worked as her father's clerk and assistant. She was brilliant,
humorous, balanced, compassionate, and terribly bored. She needed Hull-
House as much as Addams did, and she leapt eagerly at the chance to join.
Lathrop would become a major, original force in the new field of juvenile
justice. In 1893 she was appointed to the Illinois Board of Charities; she
organized the first juvenile court in the country. In 1912 she became the
first head of the new national Children's Bureau, the first such child-
focused agency in the world; she was the first woman ever appointed to
head a Federal bureau.

Florence Kelley, a year older than Addams, arrived on the doorstep of
Hull-House in a snowstorm at Christmas time of 1891. She had grown
from much the same soil as Addams and Lathrop. Kelley's father, a fervent
Lincoln supporter with a Quaker background, was a judge in Philadelphia;
he thoroughly supported her thirst for education. Kelley attended Cornell
University, a secular institution with radical leanings, one of the few
major colleges that accepted women. Angry and frustrated when she was
denied admission to the University of Pennsylvania Law School, she es-
caped to Europe and enrolled at the University of Zurich, the first European university to admit female doctoral candidates. Kelley became a
socialist and a friend of Friedrich Engels (Karl Marx's writing partner),
and even translated Engels into English. She married a Polish physician
and settled in New York with their three small children. The marriage

soon foundered, and Kelley moved to Chicago in 1891, seeking divorce laws more equitable than New York State's.

Florence Kelley's personality and her brand of social and political activism—utterly determined and ferociously well-informed—brought a radically different perspective to Hull-House. She had been married and had children; she had worked on economic issues with a scientific, statistical expertise new to the other residents. Even more, she brought a fierce, unflinchingly class-oriented understanding of the myriad conflicts faced by poor workers. Addams mistrusted dogmas and labels, and she tried to avoid the larger structural implications of her own work, but there is no doubt that Kelley's drive and vision profoundly altered the mission of Hull-House. Addams's favorite nephew, who spent a great deal of time at the house, described Kelley as "the toughest customer in the reform riot, the finest rough-and-tumble fighter for the good life for others, that Hull-House ever knew. Any weapon was a good weapon in her hand—evidence, argument, irony or invective" (Linn [1935] 2000, 138).

Kelley assumed command of Hull-House's Bureau of Labor. In 1892 she was appointed by the state Commissioner of Commerce and Labor to conduct research on sweatshops in Chicago; she investigated over 2,500 such shops in the city, some exploiting children as young as three for 12-hour, 7-day weeks. Outraged, Florence Kelley declared war. She wrote a factory inspection bill and relentlessly guided it through the state legislature. In 1893 Governor John Peter Altgeld (already notorious because he had pardoned the surviving Haymarket Martyrs) appointed Kelley the first chief factory inspector authorized under the new legislation. Working full-time, Kelley attended Northwestern University Law School at night and received her law degree in 1894. Julia Lathrop was known as a diplomat, but Kelley was a warrior. She was a vital, intimidating presence at Hull-House until 1899, when she returned to New York City to head the newly formed National Consumers League.

Kelley remained a close ally for Addams, committed but willing to provoke and criticize, one of the few around Addams who could temper her respect with humor. At one point, referring to an annoyingly effusive woman, Kelley muttered to Addams, "Do you know what I would do if that woman calls you a saint again? I'd show her my teeth, and if that didn't convince her, I would bite her" (Linn [1935] 2000, 139). Addams missed her keenly; she wrote to Kelley shortly after she left, "Hull-House sometimes seems a howling wilderness without you" (Sklar 1990, 111).

Addams, Lathrop, and Kelley were the glowing furnace that animated the rest of Hull-House. They were in many ways, despite their assorted

ambitions, education, and quirks, well-bred Victorian ladies who treasured their own privacy and dignity and had great consideration for the
privacy of others. Their respect and affection for each other was open and
obvious; in correspondence Kelley referred to Addams as "Beloved Lady."
But they called each Miss Addams, Miss Lathrop, Sister Kelley; they kept
careful boundaries and did not trespass on each other's privacy.

Mary Kenny was another remarkable member of the self-selected family of Hull-House. A tall Irishwoman four years younger than Addams,
she had left school at the age of 10 to work as a seamstress's apprentice.
She moved into bookbinding and printing, and quickly became involved
in the Chicago labor movement; she organized the first women's bookbinding union in the city. When she was invited to join Hull-House, she
worried about the enormous class gulf between her and the other residents. Addams invited Kenny's union to use Hull-House as a meeting
place, and she offered to work with Kenny to improve the conditions of
the binders' lives. Kenny was convinced of Addams's sincerity. "It was
that work 'with' from Jane Addams that took the bitterness out of my life.
For if she wanted to work *with* me and I could work with her, it gave my
life new meaning and hope" (Davis 1973, 79). Kenny played a critical role
in bringing other working girls to Hull-House; she worked with them to
start a safe, cooperative boarding house. She helped lobby the state legislature for Kelley's factory inspection bill, and served as a deputy inspector
under Kelley's supervision. Kenny's presence and perspective pushed Addams toward an active effort to attack the causes of poverty. Although she
soon married and moved to Boston, she would be a regular visitor to Hull-
House for the rest of her life.

Alzina Stevens was 11 years older than Addams and represented yet
another profoundly different world that could still be welcomed and embraced at Hull-House. Born in rural Maine, Stevens had been sent at the
age of 13 to work in a textile mill; an accident there had ripped off her
right index finger. Her mutilated hand became a constant symbol of the
vulnerability of working children, of society's responsibility to protect the
defenseless. Stevens found her way to Chicago, where she worked as a
typesetter and became the first president of the Working Woman's Union;
a firebrand in defense of labor, she could often be found marching with
strikers wherever there was a picket line. In 1899 she was appointed the
first probation officer of the new Juvenile Court in Chicago, pioneered by
Julia Lathrop.

The last to join this astonishing family was Alice Hamilton, who held a
medical degree from the University of Michigan and had done further study

at Johns Hopkins University as well as in Europe. In 1898 when she came to Chicago to work at Rush Hospital, she became a resident at Hull-House. Hamilton was a dedicated scientist, gentle and deeply humorous. As a physician she was in an ideal position to watch over and advise Addams, whose health was somewhat precarious and who was known to work herself into exhaustion. As far as other residents could tell, Hamilton issued many health directives to Addams, few of which were obeyed. Hamilton soon became a professor of pathology at the Women's Medical College of Northwestern University. She investigated the physiological impact of various environmental factors within the Hull-House neighborhood, wrote a textbook on the dangerous professions, and is generally credited with founding the field of industrial medicine. In 1919 Hamilton was appointed professor of industrial medicine at Harvard Medical School; although she left Chicago at this point, she maintained close connections with the women of Hull-House. A deeply committed pacifist, she would be an integral player in the women's peace efforts during and after the First World War.

All the talent and commitment in the world could not have ensured the survival of Hull-House without sufficient financial support. Addams herself dedicated her income to the project, but even her relative wealth could cover only one-half the budget. There were thousands of small individual donations, but the sheer scope of the endeavor called for larger, sustained support. One major benefactor was Louise de Koven Bowen, the wife of a wealthy businessman in Chicago. Born to great privilege, Bowen would never become a resident of Hull-House, but she used her power and influence to nurture the settlement and its dreams; it is probable that without Louise Bowen, Hull-House would not have survived. Bowen was as blunt and confrontational as Florence Kelley. She was generous but imperious, and Addams was frequently called upon to soothe her feathers when someone less tactful had ruffled them. Despite the difficulties, Bowen's support was essential and extensive. She financed several new buildings for the rapidly expanding compound that was Hull-House. She donated 72 acres of beautiful rolling countryside in Waukegan, on the North Shore of Lake Michigan, as a summer location for residents and neighbors. Bowen's influence helped push Lathrop's juvenile court proposal through the city bureaucracy. When the city finally established a juvenile court, it provided no salaries for the officers appointed; Bowen contributed much of the money for those salaries, and she personally raised the remainder from her own friends.

The character of the Hull-House family was further enriched by the graceful presence of Mary Rozet Smith, the youngest early member and the absolute archetype of the wealthy, educated, aimless young woman for whom Hull-House represented salvation. Smith's father was a powerful industrialist, her mother an icon of Philadelphia society. Smith was reasonably well educated and had traveled extensively in Europe. She was drawn to Hull-House through a close friend who was the first kindergarten teacher at the settlement; she was enchanted, and she was intimately involved with the house and the family for the rest of her life. As James Linn remembered her, "She was barely 20; tall, shy, fair, and eager. From that day until she died, 43 years later, the interests of the House remained the center of her own interests, and the friendship of Mary Smith soon became and always remained the highest and clearest note in the music that was Jane Addams's personal life" (Linn [1935] 2000, 147). Smith made major, crucial donations of her own money, and she convinced her father to contribute even more. Later, as a trustee, she provided sensitive social guidance as well as unstinting financial support. Smith even nurtured Florence Kelley's children, paying their college tuition long after Kelley had returned to New York. But her greatest gift was the utterly uncritical, constant love she offered Jane Addams.

Addams and Smith became inseparable. They traveled together, took vacations together; Smith probably paid the greater share for the home near Bar Harbor, Maine, where the two spent summers from 1905 on. In Chicago, Smith's family embraced Addams warmly, and she spent a great deal of time with them. In later years, as life at Hull-House became ever more hectic and public, Addams was more likely to stay with the Smiths when she was in Chicago. Mary Smith devoted herself almost exclusively to the care and maintenance of Jane Addams.

What was the nature of their relationship? Their letters to each other are passionate and loving, often poignant with the ache of separation. (Mary saved every letter she ever received from Jane, but Jane destroyed most of Mary's.) They referred to themselves as an old married couple, and Addams noted the "healing domesticity" of their lives together. Addams's niece, Marcet Haldeman-Julius, wrote after Addams's death, "The love and understanding between them was so limitless that Miss Smith could and did furnish Aunt Jane with a tender, tonic criticism that she found nowhere else" (Haldeman-Julius 1936, 10). Clearly, this was the central emotional relationship in both their lives. Was it sexual as well, and was it consummated? There is no way to know, and the question itself serves no purpose. Addams was an intensely private person; her public persona radiated great warmth that also seemed to set a distance, to establish a limited degree of acceptable intimacy. Only Ellen Starr and later, even more strongly, Mary Rozet Smith, were ever invited past the barrier of that reserve. It is significant that Smith enriched, encouraged, and inspired Addams, that Addams could go forth from the loving privacy of their relationship to write, act, and exhort as she did. Does it further our understanding of either of them to posit conjectural details of that relationship?

The first residents of Hull-House were all women, but by late 1891 the settlement was accepting male residents. Eventually, men would make up one-third of all residents, but they never moved into central positions of authority. Hull-House remained an invaluable hub of shared understanding and support from which women reformers could operate without the dominance of male associations. As the energy of the Progressive Era gathered momentum, these women recognized that they were part of a vibrant alternative network of women's associations, well educated, well financed, well informed.

Hull-House was an instant social success. The early popular reaction was overwhelmingly positive. Glowing, highly sentimental articles about Addams and Starr appeared in newspapers, women's magazines, and even the *New York World* before they had even moved in. Ironically, such popular acclaim did not serve Addams well: the lavish praise squeezed her into the mold of conventional imagery as a pious, spiritual, chaste Christian icon of sacrifice. The focus was on Addams and Starr as individual actors, as sort of vicarious agents of goodness whose very activities allowed the middle and upper classes to avoid any confrontation with their own consciences and with any concept of collective responsibility for the awful conditions Hull-House was attempting to ameliorate. Among the actual residents of the district, reactions were more varied and guarded. Most immigrants' dealings with native-born Americans involved frequently unpleasant, demeaning interchanges with assorted bureaucrats, slumlords, impatient bosses, intimidating health officers; there was no implicit reason to trust these strange, well-dressed young women who had moved into that big old house without proper chaperones. Hull-House would have to prove itself to the suspicious community.

Within months the number of residents jumped from the original 3 to 6, to 15, and soon to 20. Eager young women were clamoring for rooms faster than those rooms could be outfitted for them. As Addams reported to her sister Mary, a supportive man from a highly respected mission told her that she "voiced something hundreds of young people in the city were trying to express, and that he could send us three young ladies at once who possessed both money and a knowledge of Herbert Spencer's 'Sociology,' but who are dying from inaction and restlessness" (JAMSS). Residents participated in and initiated a broad spectrum of activities at Hull-House: reading groups, reading aloud to children and illiterate adults, political and philosophical debate, cooking classes, nursing instruction, childcare, and many others.

The immediate impact of Hull-House is difficult to comprehend. Hull-House was the first settlement in Chicago, and the first in the entire United States to accept both men and women as residents. It pioneered the first public playground in Chicago, the first public gymnasium, the first public baths in a neighborhood where hygiene was in a state of constant crisis. The women of Hull-House opened the first community theater in the United States, the first citizenship preparation classes anywhere in America, the first public kitchen in Chicago, the city's first public swimming pool, Boy Scout troop, college extension classes. Both Addams and Starr were deeply convinced that the arts could play a central role in ennobling the lives of both residents and guests. The first major gift to Hull-House was used to build an art gallery, which opened in 1891. That first year Hull-House welcomed 50,000 visitors; by the next year the number had risen to 2,000 each week.

Addams was ecstatically, exhaustingly busy. She handled the fundraising, public speaking, bookkeeping; she made numerous home visits, helped lay out the dead, once delivered an illegitimate baby whose desperate mother had been abandoned by her shamed family. And always, she was the vital, welcoming sun around which the rest of the Hull-House solar system revolved. A childhood visitor to Hull-House recounted, "Miss Addams was essentially a housekeeper. Hull-House was her home and she had a passion for changing furniture.... I never knew which was more amazing—this delightful joy in housekeeping, or her passion for riding fast in an automobile.... To us, these surprises in her personality were always among her greatest charms" (Detzer 1938, 4). A Greek immigrant boy recalled how he and his friends had wandered in absolute freedom within Hull-House, drinking in the gentle, nurturing conversation of the ladies of the house, "the only soft and kind words we immigrant boys heard in those days." But Addams was never in really robust health, and she drove herself hard to keep up with the magnificent purpose she had created for herself. Louis Bowen confessed years later, "She impressed me then as always being very sad, as if the sorrows of the neighborhood were pressing upon her, which indeed they were" (Linn [1935] 2000, 111, 435).

Hull-House operated as a loose parliamentary democracy. Weekly meetings of all the residents set fees for room and board, voted on potential new residents, decided on projects, assigned tasks and articulated expectations. The assorted clubs, classes, and teams nurtured at Hull-House—even the children's activities—were largely self-governing bodies with constitutions and voting members. They were living evidence of Addams's commitment to social democracy functioning at the most local level. Addams herself chaired the residents' meetings, and she tried at first not to exert too much overt control. Her style combined great attention to individuals with the same reserved, almost abstracted quality that was an intrinsic part of her personality. Alice Hamilton recalled:

> Most great women are surrounded by a crowd of devoted friends and admirers and Jane Addams had her share, but she would not permit too close an approach, she never encouraged the sort of loving protection that so many prominent women have offered them. She was warn and approachable, but we did not dare to refuse her to callers, no matter how tired she might be, or take her telephone calls. She kept an impersonal atmosphere in Hull-House, which is unusual for a place dominated by women. (Hamilton 1955, 2)

Hull-House seemed to function as an incubator for activists, a seedbed for new professions including schools of social work, juvenile courts, children's bureaus, and industrial medicine. Addams herself never became a professional at anything, and she was always wary of the dehumanizing dangers of professionalization. Her insistence on reciprocity and mutuality in the life of Hull-House residents and neighbors precluded any sense of a practitioner-client relationship. The settlement, she wrote in 1899, "stands for application and research; for universal interest, as opposed to specialization" (Miller and Cimbala 1996, 7).

Many of Hull-House's supporters saw the settlement through the lens of the Social Gospel Movement, which grew out of an awareness of the terrible inequities of urban life in industrialized America, and argued that true Christianity had to be lived in acts of daily justice, not merely in the rituals of Sunday observance. There were certainly many points of ethical overlap, but there were also points of divergence. The benevolence of the Social Gospel was easily tainted by righteousness and condescension to the poor, which Addams rejected vehemently. Addams spoke often of the transcendent aspect of the human spirit, of ways to nurture the highest and most noble impulses and attitudes in human nature; she could sound at times almost mystical. But her concerns were always grounded in people's relationships to each other, not to God. At first there were evening Bible readings at Hull-House, but the core family of residents (with the exception of Starr) were an utterly secular group of women, and overtly religious activities died out quickly. There was no religious instruction at Hull-House. Addams's real faith was in the possibility of democracy and in the openness of conscience to reason and education. One scholar has described Hull-House as "a political boat on a religious stream, advancing political solutions to social problems that were fundamentally ethical or moral..." (Sklar 1990, 112). This determinedly nonreligious flavor was distasteful to some. A 1903 editorial in the *Chicago Chronicle* blasted Hull-House for hosting the renowned socialist Eugene V. Debs, who had allegedly declared Karl Marx greater than Thomas Jefferson. The *Chronicle* suggested that if Hull-House found it "inconvenient" to do its work with any religious connections, the work was perhaps not worth doing in the first place.

Even before the transformative arrival of Florence Kelley, Addams was drawn to radical solutions to the problems of labor. She was intrigued by anarchism, a political philosophy that, in its rejection of all government, could seem to place the greatest faith possible in the benevolence of human nature. Within months of opening Hull-House, Addams invited a libertarian group in Chicago to meet there; they discussed the work of the Russian anarchist Prince Peter Kropotkin, who declared unequivocally that true anarchism celebrated all aspects of growth and deplored any violence. Despite her disguise as a genteel, young, middle-class spinster, Addams was drawn to unpopular causes and positions all her life.

Addams always tried to believe that compromise and conciliation were preferable to conflict. In a paradoxical way, her faith in compromise became a principle in itself. Her eminent social respectability; her gentle, patient demeanor; her moderate tone; and her refusal to accept labels imposed by others all allowed her to function as a great facilitator: she could draw disparate people together, offer them space and time and a calm sense of being heard, encourage them to listen to each other. Hull-House hosted a range of prominent reform-minded figures from all classes and many ideological stances, among them the progressive economist Henry Demarest Lloyd, the great defense lawyer Clarence Darrow, the working-class union activist Abraham Bisno.

By 1892 Hull-House offered 35 evening college-extension classes a week. A low-rent cooperative boardinghouse for working girls (the Jane Club) occupied an entire nearby building and offered safe living quarters for more than 50 young women, Typically, Addams herself had paid the first month's rent on the first two apartments in the new venture, but shortly thereafter the club was self-sustaining; it was the first such living experiment in the United States founded and managed by women. The Diet Kitchen, in consultation with doctors and visiting nurses, prepared special meals for homebound invalids, which were delivered by neighborhood volunteers. The residents organized a coal-buying cooperative to keep fuel costs down. Hull-House now offered five bathing rooms open to the public, which were in constant use; 980 poor neighbors enjoyed baths there in the month of July alone. A new six-room cottage on the property provided daycare for 40 children each day.

Addams always insisted that none of this was, strictly speaking, charity or philanthropy; rather, the learning and enrichment were always mutual. She argued that the working poor neither wanted nor needed charity; they needed opportunities to take charge of their lives, and justice required that society provide those opportunities. "Hull-House makes a constant effort to secure these means for its neighbors, but to call that effort philanthropy is to use the word unfairly and to underestimate the duties of good citizenship" (Addams 1965, 61). "It was the function of settlements," she wrote many years later, "to bring into the circle of knowledge and fuller life, men and women who might otherwise be left outside" (Addams 1935, 404). Surely this statement refers to the economic and cultural deprivation of the poor; but just as surely, Addams had seen herself before Hull-House, and other women like her, as standing outside the circle of meaningful life.

Chapter 4

WIDENING SPHERES

With Hull-House in the 1890s, Jane Addams had dropped an amazing pebble into the waters of American social and political life. Its impact and influence radiated in startling, often unanticipated ripples out from 335 South Halstead Street across the city, the state, the nation, and even beyond. At the center of it all Addams, who had after all started out looking for a way to find some meaning for herself, grew rapidly into a nationally recognized lecturer and writer, a spokesperson for numerous causes, a labor mediator, and a celebrity of rock-star dimensions. Throughout her life Addams consistently emphasized the primal nurturing role of Woman toward her children and family—and just as consistently, Addams's definition of family expanded to transcend the genetic and national, to embrace all children and all families. That kind of embrace demanded an increasingly broad activist role in helping to make life bearable and safe for all the world's children.

Living at Hull-House, observing her neighbors' lives in intimate detail, meeting the laborers whose union meetings Hull-House hosted, Addams learned more than she might have first expected. The quality of the immigrants' lives was in so many ways beyond their control, no matter what standards they understood and tried to observe. No one could stay clean and healthy or keep a clean apartment in a district where plumbing and sewer services were minimal, food delivery was careless and unsanitary, and garbage removal was sporadic at best. At first the residents of Hull-House saw themselves as ombudsmen communicating with local authorities on behalf of their less articulate neighbors. During the summer of 1892 Hull-House filed 1,037 complaints with the City Health Depart-

ment, citing specific local sanitary violations; there were noticeable improvements in some services, at least for a while.

It was important for these genteel, well-bred women to realize that organized protest could be effective in demanding that certain regulations
be enforced, but more significant was the recognition that situations of
chronic abuse and exploitation called for new laws. The Depression of
1893 thrust Hull-House into a prominent role in relief and reform efforts.
The house became the district headquarters for the Central Relief Association, distributing coal, clothing, and fuel to desperate families. Addams's membership on the five-person citywide Civic Federation
committee was the first public position any of the Hull-House residents
had undertaken. It was only the beginning of their civic involvement.

Florence Kelley spearheaded Hull-House's monumental research on
sweatshops and living conditions in the slums. With the support of John
Peter Altgeld, the newly elected, reform-minded governor of Illinois, Kelley conducted a highly systematic, scientific survey of factories, child
labor, and living conditions in Chicago. Supported by her own appalling
data, Kelley designed Illinois' first anti-sweatshop law, which raised the
legal age of employment to 14 and limited women to an 8-hour day. Altgeld appointed Kelley the state's first chief inspector, with an assistant and
a staff of 10 deputies. Alzina Stevens of Hull-House was Kelley's assistant;
the prosecuting attorney who handled many of their cases was Alexander
Bruce, who also lived at Hull-House. If industrialists and bankers wanted
to imagine a conspiracy of pro-labor activism emanating from Hull-
House, one can scarcely blame them.

Kelley's research was published in 1895 as *Hull-House Maps and Papers*,
the first such statistical survey in the United States. Ironically, that same
year the Illinois Supreme Court struck down the factory reform law as an
infringement on the "freedom of contract" (that is, workers' right to be
exploited). Altgeld, much reviled since he had pardoned the surviving
Haymarket anarchists, lost his bid for reelection in 1896 to a conservative
candidate. The new governor promptly fired Kelley and assigned in her
place a former factory superintendent who had himself been convicted of
safety violations.

Addams's relationship with Altgeld is a good indicator of the depth of
her loyalty and courage. Altgeld's public career and much of his private
life were devastated when he pardoned the three surviving anarchists
from the 1886 Haymarket Riot. When he died in 1902, a shunned and despised figure, his funeral was a stark affair; a minister officiated, and the
only mourners present were his controversial law partner, Clarence Dar-

row, and Jane Addams of Hull-House. Many friends had warned Addams not to taint her own reputation—and by extension to jeopardize donations to Hull-House—by speaking at the funeral, but she had respected Altgeld deeply and she refused to abandon him in death.

One of Addams's central goals was the elimination of child labor. She recognized the complex economic equations of poverty, in which a child's meager wages might be an essential variable, might mean that a family didn't have to choose between eating and paying the rent. However, children were paid so much less than adults that child labor weakened any wage demands adult workers could make. Ultimately, it was better for the children and the adults if children could leave the shops and mills and go to school. As minimal as legal limitations on child labor were in the 1890s, factory owners could usually ignore them with impunity. Addams was determined not to let that happen. After Addams's death, Dorothy Detzer, who as a young woman had almost grown up at Hull-House, told a vivid story of Addams's response to child labor: "There are many who have told of Miss Addams's humor, of her gentleness, of her brilliance, of her great human heart. But I have never heard anyone speak of another quality which to me was one of the most stimulating and challenging characteristics of this greatest woman of our times. I refer to her anger." In this anecdote, Addams discovered a weeping, abused child on the porch of Hull-House late one evening. The little girl told Addams that she worked a night shift at a nut-shelling factory nearby; she had fallen asleep at work, been beaten by her father, and had run away. Addams went immediately to the chief of the Juvenile Protective Association (whose offices were at Hull-House). Detzer accompanied her on her mission: "Led by a little girl, I went with the officers who raided 23 secret nut-shelling factories which employed and exploited children. And as we swept through the streets of that great, sprawling city, Miss Addams's anger rode with me in the police patrol—that driving emotion stirred by injustice, which can change a world!" (Detzer 1938, 5).

There was great labor unrest throughout the 1890s, union organizing, repression by owners, strikes and frequently violent reprisals against workers, often carried out with all the might of the state and Federal government. Addams tried to function as a conciliator; with her enormous faith in the possibility of understanding, she tried to find solutions both management and workers could live with. She defended the legitimate demands of labor but did not hesitate to denounce corruption and violence within the workers' ranks. She condemned selfishness and indifference among the bosses, but stopped short of blaming capitalism and the profit motive. Unlike Ellen

Starr, she never actually walked a picket line with strikers; she was neither as polemic nor as aggressive as Florence Kelley. Under those circumstances, it is not surprising that both sides could distrust her. The mainstream press began to portray her as too pro-labor and dangerously radical; editorials demanded that she stop hosting union meetings at Hull-House. Addams herself rejected the socialist or radical label; her most radical posture in those years was her unwavering support for freedom of speech and the free exchange of ideas. Many in the labor movement saw her as too bourgeoisie, too accommodating, too trusting. Her careful, polite demeanor could mask a fierce determination to maintain her own ethical independence. A friend recalled a potentially difficult moment when Addams was addressing a group of disgruntled laborers on the needs and rights of working women; an angry heckler in the crowd accosted her: " 'You are all right now, sister, but mark my words, when you are subsidized by millionaires, you will be afraid to talk like this.' Miss Addams, so the story goes, replied that while she did not intend to be subsidized by millionaires, neither did she propose to be bullied by workingmen, and that she would state her honest opinion without consulting either of them. To her surprise, the audience of radicals broke into applause" (Gilman 1948, 4).

By 1894 the Pullman Palace Car Company in Pullman, Illinois, the major manufacturer of railroad passenger cars, had inflicted five successive pay reductions on its workers. Despite a superficially pretty company town in which workers rented pretty houses from Pullman, shopped in Pullman's company store, and attended appropriately uplifting theatrical performances in the town auditorium, the despairing workers struck, supported by the American Railway Union, which had just won a major strike against the Great Northern Railway under the inspired leadership of Eugene V. Debs. The union declared a sympathy strike with the Pullman workers and boycotted all Pullman cars. Across America, railroad companies fired workers who refused to handle Pullman cars, and the union's strike spread to other railways. Railroad traffic—the major form of industrial transport in the late nineteenth century—ground to a standstill. In the era before widespread use of the automobile, the country was virtually paralyzed. Over the vehement objections of Governor Altgeld, President Grover Cleveland sent Federal troops to help Pullman's private army defeat the strikers. The complacent middle class was shocked by the level of rage and resentment among the workers. After all, George M. Pullman was much touted as the model employer, full of enlightened benevolence, and Pullman, Illinois, was supposed to be the ideal company town in which paternalism uplifted the lives of workers who were—well, working-class.

Jane Addams was horrified on many levels by the violence that erupted. She wrote a scathing article entitled "A Modern Lear," which compared Pullman's blindness to that of King Lear. Just as Lear was unable to recognize his daughter Cordelia's independence and maturity, she argued, Pullman and other industrialists refused to see the scale of the world-wide labor movement, "the force and power of this movement... that conception of duty which induces men to go without food and to see their wives and children suffer for the sake of securing better wages for fellow-workmen whom they have never seen..." However strenuously Addams may have avoided political and philosophical labels, she utilized a socialist vocabulary in her analysis of what had happened at Pullman. She referred to the workers as the proletariat, and she spoke of the "subordination of individual and trade interests to the good of the working class" (Addams 1965, 115). She read this paper to the Women's Club in Chicago and to the influential Twentieth Century Club in Boston, but her friends and associates considered it too angry and outspoken to publish; the *Survey*, the national journal of the progressive settlement movement, finally published "A Modern Lear" in 1912. Addams portrayed George Pullman as a misguided, deluded Lear, giving his "children" what *he* thought they needed, stunned by their rebellion; she described Lear's relationship to his daughters as "archaic and barbaric" and declared that "industrial relationships"—that is, the treatment of workers—were equally primitive and undeveloped. Indeed, reacting to Pullman's greed and insensitivity and to the brutality of the Federal troops, the strikers displayed astonishing discipline and control. Despite overwhelming provocation, there was no destruction of company property: when the Pullman company billed the city of Chicago for damages after the strike, all it could invent was $26.00 as a result of minor accidents. To Addams, the tragedy stemmed from Pullman's arrogant failure to consult with his workers, to see them as real people and to inquire about their desires and sense of their own needs. This failure was in turn rooted in the profit system, in which Pullman's sense of his own right to an arbitrary four percent profit drove him to cut wages with no thoughts to the real lives of his real workers. This was everything Addams abhorred: even the highly touted benevolence of the company town was a doing good for rather than with: "The absolute authority of this employer over his town [is] a typical and dramatic example of the industrial tragedy" (Addams 1965, 111).

By the early 1900s Addams was frequently denounced in Chicago newspapers as a socialist, as a supporter of anarchists, too pro-labor, not a proper Christian. While some socialist critics also denounced her as too conservative, they recognized her invaluable middle-class connections and treasured the unflagging concern for individual human beings she always demonstrated. In the fall of 1909 a spontaneous walkout of garment workers, largely female, grew quickly into the largest strike in Chicago history. The strike started at the shops of Hart, Schaffner, and Marx and involved a reduction in the already abysmal piecework rate; general anger over wages and working conditions snowballed into a strike involving over 40,000 workers throughout Chicago. Ellen Starr joined the picket lines, where she literally got her hands dirty and faced real danger: while the police stood by idly, thugs hired by the bosses beat up the young striking women. Addams didn't picket, but she organized a relief fund for the strikers' families; she met and befriended Sidney Hillman, the dynamic young leader of the garment workers' union. In the balancing act that was Addams's world, she was friendly as well with both Harry Hart and Joseph Schaffner, the shop owners, both of whom were Hull-House donors; Addams was able to advocate for the strikers over dinner at Hart's house. While the strike resulted in a partial victory for the workers, Addams was left off the arbitration board because both sides distrusted her a little. In the words of Walter Rauschenbush, a leading Social Gospel minister, "You are one of the invaluable people who combine velocity and stability, so that conservatives have to remain respectful toward you even while they are being dragged along" (Davis 1973, 119).

Hull-House was in many profound ways not a representative settlement. In its emphasis on each individual resident's direct responsibility for self-development as a vehicle for broader social change, it reflected Jane Addams's own journey and commitment. The house thrived on this complex balance of individual and community, of an overarching faith in human growth that was at the same time grounded in practical responses to specific situations and needs. Something at Hull-House spawned a level of energy, creativity, and ethical commitment unmatched anywhere else. One elderly woman, interviewed in the 1990s, recalled with awe the gracious world of possibilities that Hull-House had offered her 80 years earlier: "It was a way of life. You walked through the door, and things happened...Hull-House introduced us to so many things. It was such a rich environment. That's what everybody has forgotten" (Elshtain 2002, 9).

By 1895 Hull-House was formally incorporated with a dedicated board of trustees. Addams was still head resident and was elected president of the Hull-House Association year after year. She was really the manager, treasurer, secretary, and almost everything else. She had become a shrewd businesswoman, a seasoned fundraiser with a relentless follow-up technique, a hand-holder, publicist, negotiator, public speaker. Hull-House attracted an international, prestigious guest list that included crusading English journalists, Fabian socialists, leading politicians, and even the anarchist Peter Kropotkin. Addams was especially pleased by a visit by the Reverend Samuel Barnett, the head resident at Toynbee Hall who had so inspired her.

Through all the growing acclaim, Addams never lost sight of the particular moments that called for action. One of the worst problems in the neighborhood was the erratic and inadequate garbage removal. In 1895, when conventional complaints had brought no relief, Addams actually submitted a bid for the contract to haul garbage from the ward. Her willingness quite literally to get her hands dirty horrified and delighted the newspapers. Her bid was dismissed, but the mayor appointed her garbage inspector for the ward, a paid position with a salary of $1,000 a year. She kept the job for under a year, and she was unable to make a substantial difference at it, but the publicity was enormous. Her brother was mortified; he cabled her, "Jane, please draw the line on garbage" (Gilman 1948, 2). But that was really the point: Addams didn't draw the line at garbage. In social activism, she never quite stayed behind any line; while she seemed often to observe the conventions, in many instances she simply dragged that line with her where she felt it needed to go.

It is probably impossible to overstate the extent of Hull-House's impact on the delivery of social services. Julia Lathrop was instrumental in developing the School of Civics and Social Philanthropy of Chicago Commons, which was soon taken over by the new University of Chicago. It became the Graduate School of Social Service Administration; the dean of the school was Edith Abbott, a Hull-House resident, and the executive officer was Sophonisba Breckenridge, another long-time resident. Hull-House was involved with the University of Chicago from its inception. The great American philosopher John Dewey stopped to visit Hull-House in 1892 before he accepted a job offer from the University; as a devoted supporter of Addams and later a trustee of Hull-House, Dewey brought many colleagues into the eclectic world of the settlement. The University soon opened its own settlement, headed by Mary MacDowell, a dear friend of Addams. Other universities across the country followed suit. Years later another prominent University professor, who had as a young man lived at Hull-House for sixteen years, spoke of the weight of Hull-House's example: "In fact, it came to be quickly recognized that a university settlement was part of the apparatus of an institution of higher learning..." (Lovett 1946, 10). All these settlements wielded enormous influence in shaping the professions of sociology and public administration; they provided constant reality checks against which academics and practitioners could observe the value of theory and abstraction.

In 1893 Addams was appointed to the Chicago School Board. It was a tumultuous time for education in Chicago: there was a growing sense of professionalism among public school teachers, who used a fledgling union to demand recognition, pensions, tenure, and better salaries. That same taste of possibility led to a willingness to experiment with more progressive educational methods that were not always well received by the general public. The new school board supported teachers' rights, awarded higher salaries, investigated the inadequate corporate tax structure. Mainstream newspapers labeled the Board dangerously socialist. Addams was chair of the School Management Committee, responsible for issues of curriculum, salaries, standards for promotion, and supplies. In her efforts to listen to everyone in disputes, to try to find common ground, she sometimes angered all the parties involved. Is it possible that Addams's best role as a gadfly to the social conscience called for an outsider's perspective? Was she less effective when she joined the system?

In Jane Addams's philosophy of human connectedness, many varied strands of reform were to be woven into a fabric of justice and inclusiveness. She recognized the interdependent nature of the struggles for women's rights and civil rights. As a very young woman first entering Rockford Female Seminary, she had asserted women's right to education but had evinced only mild interest in the issue of women's suffrage. At Rockford she met Catherine Waugh, a brilliant young woman who went on to study and practice law; as Catherine Waugh McCulloch she would lead the fight for women's suffrage in Illinois. McCullough was a powerful influence on Addams, although Addams believed that the vote alone would never be enough to bring real economic and social equality to women. Believing as she did in the possibility of broadening human understanding, she sought a psychological equality for all people, which she hoped could be achieved through education and cooperation, not competition. Nonetheless, Addams believed in the power of organizing; she served as first vice-president of the National American Woman Suffrage Association from 1911–1914, and in 1913 attended the convention of the International Woman Suffrage Alliance.

In the early stages of her awareness, Addams tried to disclaim the notion that women were morally superior to men. "We have not wrecked railroads, nor corrupted legislatures, nor done many unholy things that men have done," she wrote in the *Woman's Journal* in 1897, "but then we must remember that we have not had the chance" (Davis 1973, 187). This gentle demurral, of course, was offered *before* both the Spanish-American War and the First World War. By the time the International Congress of Women convened in Zurich in 1919, Addams and many other pacifist women had lost all confidence in men's ability to manage their own tempers, let alone the rest of the world. It is equally true that Addams and many other suffragists did expect women to vote as a morally cohesive unit that would eliminate child labor, worker exploitation, and a plethora of assorted other vices. The danger in this perspective is that it can make women's suffrage seem like a means to a moral end, not an unrestricted right of itself.

Addams viewed women as a social class with distinct interests and needs that could not be fully understood or served by men. She was reluctant to recognize that women's class identifications might complicate and compromise their gender loyalties. In a way, her own fierce gender loyalty let her transcend those very class distinctions: while many middle- and upper-class reformers linked class and intelligence and would have limited suffrage to their own sort, Addams always trusted the intelligence of working-class women and insisted on their right to vote. She argued that working women especially needed the vote to help protect themselves from exploitation by wealthier women. "I have discovered," she wrote, "that the unrepresented are always liable to be given what they do not need by legislators who wish merely to placate them" (Addams 1965, 158).

There were very few African Americans in the Hull-House district until after World War I. Nonetheless, Addams became the first settlement director to invite a black resident into a settlement in a white community when Harriet Rice, a black graduate of Wellesley College and a physician, became a resident of Hull-House in 1892; Rice would live at Hull-House until 1904. Addams supported black Chicagoans in their efforts to open a settlement, and she urged the Chicago Women's Club to accept black members.

Another African American, Lugenia Burns Hope, grew up in Chicago and participated in many activities at Hull-House. She later credited Addams with offering her a coherent vision of the potential for organizing poor communities. In 1897 Hope married John Hope, a theology student, and moved to Atlanta with him; there, she helped organize a network of social services and civic projects for a substantial black population in a rigidly segregated city that provided no services for its citizens of color.

Addams was a strong early supporter of the National Association for the Advancement of Colored People (NAACP). The NAACP grew directly out of one man's horrified reaction to murderous race riots in Springfield, Illinois, in 1908. William English Walling, a socialist from a prominent Southern family, reported on the riots for the newspaper *Independent;* he concluded his article with a plea that responsible, powerful citizens support African Americans in their struggles for justice. As a result, he met in New York City with Mary White Ovington, a sociologist who had founded a model housing project for blacks; Henry Moskowitz, a Jewish social worker and leader in the progressive Ethical Culture Society; and Oswald Garrison Villard, editor of the *New York Post* and grandson of abolitionist William Lloyd Garrison. They issued the now famous Call—on Lincoln's centenary, February 12, 1909—demanding a national conference to address the inequities and dangers endured by African Americans. The Call was signed by 60 people, black and white, who represented the highest ideals and best hopes of the Progressive era. Prominent among them was Jane Addams, whose support Walling saw as essential.

Addams was on the NAACP's first executive committee, and she was a frequent contributor to its early publication, *Social Control.* She wrote scathingly of white America's racial attitudes: "Not only in the South, but everywhere in America, a strong race antagonism is asserting itself, which has modes of lawlessness and insolence. The contemptuous attitude of the so-called superior race toward the inferior results in a social segregation of each race" (Reed 1997, 9). In this struggle, as in so many others, Addams tried to offer rather than impose notions of equality and justice. Her non-confrontational style drew some doubts from Ida B. Wells-Barnett, a powerful African American activist and leader of the crusade for federal anti-lynching legislation; Wells-Barnett wondered whether Addams was committed and firm enough to engage in real battles.

Addams was always aware of her responsibilities to Hull-House itself. She knew she needed to keep her pool of wealthy white donors, many of whom, despite their liberalism in other areas, still operated under profound racist assumptions. Addams dealt with racism much as she met other challenges: her responses were personal and positive and highly specific. As a matter of principle, she tried to employ only union labor at Hull-House. When she hired an African American chef, she discovered that no union in Chicago would accept him; she arranged for him to join an integrated union in St. Louis. Disappointed as she was to recognize racism within the unions, she continued to work on their behalf, in the amazing faith that when the structures of society were more just, human beings would grow in moral stature.

In one real racial battle Addams displayed unwavering personal courage. In July 1919 Chicago erupted into three days of hideous race riots. Hull-House's largely Greek and Polish neighbors turned ferociously on African Americans in the district; by the time the mobs subsided, there were 38 fatalities, more than 500 injuries, and untold destruction areas of property. While Hull-House stood as a solid island of sanity in the midst of horror, there was real fear that the mob would storm the house to get at the black chef, Mr. Beck. The only way to protect him was to sneak him out of the city. Addams decided to go with him as a potential shield and witness; she had a car brought into the alley behind Hull-House and they rode together through the angry mob.

When the National Association of Colored Women met in Chicago, Addams invited them to lunch at Hull-House. She entertained many black leaders, including Booker T. Washington and his wife. In the poisonous racist atmosphere that permeated American society, these were radical, daring gestures. In 1908, when Mary White Ovington attended an interracial dinner of reform leaders in New York City, she received a flood of hate mail (including death threats) and was denounced from the floor of the United States Senate. Later, Addams also sought out black women leaders for the Women's Peace Party and later for the Women's International League for Peace and Freedom. Mary B. Talbert, Charlotte Atwood, and Mary F. Waring were among the women she welcomed into peace activism. Mary Church Terrell attended the women's peace congress in Zurich in 1919 with Addams and was the only woman of color in the entire conference.

While Addams's interests and involvements expanded widely during her first 20 years in Chicago, her universe revolved around 335 South Halstead Street. Hull-House continued to respond to its neighbors with creativity and compassion. In 1900 Addams established a Labor Museum at Hull-House to honor and preserve Old World crafts and traditions increasingly threatened by mass production and assimilation. The museum employed older artisans as teachers and invited people of all ages to participate in classes. Once again, the faith was in the power of education to enrich human understanding; the hope was to nurture pride in their European cultures—and in their parents and grandparents—among the younger generation of immigrants. A Russian immigrant boy from this period recalled years later, "Jane Addams had the happy faculty of liking people of diverse backgrounds. Unlike critics of the immigrants of that day, she encouraged us to build proudly on what was most valuable in our heritage..." (Davis and McCree 1969, 118). Addams viewed the immigrant poor as citizens, active agents who could, with adequate resources, effect beneficial changes in their own lives; she refused to see them as helpless, faceless clients.

This was a period of rapid expansion and optimism at Hull-House. Addams seemed to thrive on the demands made on her; her health remained stable and her energy was high. Money worries were a constant, especially after the financial panic of 1893. Addams's own income, plus income from the various shops and enterprises within Hull-House, could cover only half of the budget. A portion of the balance might come from wealthy donors, several of whom needed exquisite soothing and flattering; the rest had to come from thousands of small donations. Addams kept the records, followed the house's accounts, shepherded her difficult benefactors with a nuanced combination of tact and no-nonsense practicality. Despite the needs, she once turned down a donation of $50,000 because it came with a request that Hull-House residents stop agitating for a factory inspection law in Illinois. The work was varied but endless, and Addams demanded dedication of everyone. James Linn recalled, "It no more occurred to her to spare others than to spare herself" (Linn [1935] 2000, 119).

The atmosphere at Hull-House charmed visitors with its welcome, warmth, culture, and open-mindedness. A reporter for *American Magazine* wrote glowingly, "Through the Hull-House drawing room there passes a procession of Greek fruit vendors, university professors, mayors, aldermen, clubwomen, factory inspectors, novelists, reporters, policemen, Italian washerwomen, socialists..., big businessmen..., English members of parliament, German scientists, and sorts of conditions of men from the river wards of the city of Chicago and from the far corners of the five continents" (de Benedetti 1986, 35). Children of the struggling poor were offered a level of cultural enrichment that had nothing to do with practical survival and everything to do with spiritual survival. An Italian immigrant girl reminisced 70 years later, "We had cellists, piano players, violinists. Many concerts. We even went to dance classes with Martha Graham [a pioneer of modern dance]. Everything was the best." Her sister chimed in that Addams set the tone of respect and welcome: "Her love rubbed off on all people" (Elshtain 2002, 12).

Holidays were especially joyous. Hull-House had become everyone's neighborhood center, a place where multiple traditions could find expression. Addams's refusal to embrace one denomination exclusively herself established the scope of appreciation and diversity there. Clearly, the assumptions of middle-class Middle America were Christian and Protestant, and Christmas was likely to be the major holiday focus. As Dorothy Detzer recalled from her own childhood, "Christmas at Hull-House was an-other delightful experience. All morning Miss Addams would open her gifts which came from many parts of the world with the greatest amount of joy and appreciation. Then after dinner she would begin and give them away" (Detzer 1938, 4).

Addams had created something remarkable and original in Hull-House. The recognition growing from that achievement gave her the confidence to become a public speaker and a published author. Her evolv-ing career as a public intellectual figure would reflect the constant inter-play between the abstract and the applied that was the deep core of her personality.

Chapter 5

OUTREACH FOR
THE CAUSE(S)

In the summer of 1892 Addams was invited to speak at the School of Applied Ethics in Plymouth, Massachusetts. With great anticipation, she traveled to the conference with Julia Lathrop. She gave two papers outlining the dual motivations behind the founding of Hull-House: "The Subjective Necessity for Social Settlements" and "The Objective Value of a Social Settlement." She described in detail how the settlement fulfilled comfortable young men and women's urgent drive to be useful to others. And she delineated with great authority the grotesque inequities slum dwellers faced and how the settlement could help the poor organize to help themselves. These two papers, later published in the influential magazine *The Forum*, launched Addams's career as a writer.

At the summer school she met with women from other settlements, among them Vida Scudder and Emily Greene Balch, both professors at Wellesley College and founders of the College Settlement Association. The professional and personal recognition and camaraderie were exhilarating. Addams came away as the acknowledged spokeswoman of the settlement movement, convinced she had important things to say to a society that might be ready to listen. Over the next 40 years she would publish 10 books and over 100 magazine and journal articles. The range of Addams's intellectual interests was as great as the range of her social commitments. Her personal library included works in philosophy, sociology, history, Quaker studies, psychology, racial issues, management, hygiene and food production, and women's studies. She read Abraham Lincoln and Giuseppe Mazzini, both heroes of her father; she read George Eliot, Leo Tolstoy, the positivist philosopher August Comte, sociologist

Thorstein Veblen, the anarchist Peter Kropotkin. She constantly searched for the concrete, the application of the philosophy. "We are all uncomfortable," she wrote in "Subjective Necessity," "in regard to the sincerity of our best phrases, because we hesitate to translate our philosophy into the deed" (Addams 1965, 32).

George Eliot, perhaps the greatest Victorian woman novelist, was at the center of Addams's moral vision. Eliot's work offers strong, challenged heroines who endure great difficulties without wallowing in victimhood. The women in *Middlemarch* recognize their responsibility for their own behavior and moral growth, no matter what inner demons may complicate that growth. Eliot also eschewed standard Victorian religious piety, and her characters seek validation in a larger, unselfish goal that carries them along with it. It is no coincidence that one of the first activities at Hull-House, only weeks after the settlement opened, was a book group that read Eliot's *Romola*—in Italian, as a courtesy to the mainly Italian participants.

Addams read and wrote from the stimulating and nourishing home base of Hull-House. She drew her hope and optimism from the community collaboration she saw enacted among the residents and the people who participated in activities at Hull-House; it seemed logical to her to extrapolate from that immediate base into a world of wider possibilities: surely, with understanding and good intentions, all peoples could learn to listen to each other, work together on common problems. Whether based on her own experiences, direct observation of others, or the voluminous research and fact-finding she did, her writing is suffused with empathy, humility, and generosity. She seemed able to recognize pain and suffering without succumbing to hopelessness.

Addams usually based an article on a speech she had given somewhere, full of rich anecdotal observations, firmly grounded in the particular. She would gradually refine it, and write it out in longhand before having it typed by someone at Hull-House. In those unthinkable days before computers, she would take scissors to the typed manuscript, cut it to ribbons, and reorganize it with straight pins. Multiple speeches on similar topics, enriched by painstaking research, would be gathered into topical books, among them *Democracy and Social Ethics* (1902), *Newer Ideals of Peace* (1907), *The Spirit of Youth and the City Streets* (1909), the famous *Twenty Years at Hull-House* (1910), and *Peace and Bread in Time of War* (1922).

In *Democracy and Social Ethics*, her first book, Addams articulated, perhaps for the first time, that the working class had its own distinct culture with values that may differ from those of a middle-class social worker. She insisted on seeing the poor within the context of their own customs, which were not implicitly inferior to those of the middle class. In fact, she wrote radically, the "money-earning capacity" so admired and rewarded in the middle-class should not be taken as any indication of high moral qualities.

The book evoked a stunning national response. The dean of American pragmatic philosophers, William James, wrote to Addams, "The religion of democracy needs nothing so much as sympathetic interpretation of one to another of the different classes of which society exists; and you have made your contribution in a masterly manner" (JAMSS). Fremont Olden, the reform editor of the San Francisco *Bulletin,* credited Addams with completely changing his assumptions about the poor: "Your psychology of the minds of the poor has been by far the most helpful aid I have ever known.... I did not understand them as you do, and as you have taught me to understand them" (JAMSS).

The glowing response to her first book impressed even Addams. She was in great demand throughout the country as a speaker and presenter at conferences. She saw herself as a sociologist, as a real scholar; she enjoyed speaking on college campuses. Although she never took an advanced degree, the University of Chicago twice offered her faculty appointments; she turned them both down. In fact, Addams warned against the influence of what she perceived as sterile academic learning: "Let the settlement people recognize the value of their own calling, and see to it that the university does not swallow the settlement, and turn it into one more laboratory: another place in which to analyze and depict, to observe and record" (Addams 1965, 196). She was always animated by both clear-eyed dismay at unjust, dangerous situations and profound faith that an education based on response to real situations could bring well-intentioned, reasonable people to better understanding of their responsibilities to each other. Her philosophy had grave difficulties recognizing people who were neither well intentioned nor reasonable.

In 1896, while traveling in Europe with Mary Rozet Smith, Addams arranged to visit Tolstoy at his vast country estate in Russia, where the great author had retreated to live an ascetic life among his peasants. Addams was impressed by Tolstoy's pacifism and the severe purity of the life he had chosen as a radical Christian. When she got back to Chicago, she even made some gestures toward a life of daily labor with her neighbors: she spent several early mornings in the kitchens of Hull-House struggling to knead bread dough for the residents. It did not take long to realize that her real skills lay elsewhere, in organization, outreach, and communication; she could even detect a sort of selfish playacting in trying to turn herself into a laborer. Tolstoy, as she came to believe, had found peace only for himself. He had removed himself from what he recognized as a corrupt system, but he had no interest in trying to change the system. Addams and the other Hull-House residents did seek such change.

After her own frustrated educational dreams, Addams was wary of the external and abstract qualities of conventional formal education. She viewed education as a shared experience, a mutual interaction between teacher and pupil from which both parties learned; this was the foundation on which she had conceived Hull-House. Her ultimate goal was to improve the quality of life for as many people as possible; the value of knowledge lay in practical applications that could enrich real people's real lives. "The settlement stands for application as opposed to research," she wrote in 1899, "for emotion as opposed to abstraction, for universal interest as opposed to specialization" (Addams 1965, 187). She believed that the validity of any idea could not be separated from its consequences, a very American, Progressive-era stance she shared both with William James and with John Dewey.

It was not surprising that Addams found a sympathetic friend in John Dewey, the great proponent of pragmatic philosophy and experiential, child-centered learning. Dewey had visited Hull-House in 1892 even before he accepted a professorship at the newly established University of Chicago. He and his wife were both actively involved at Hull-House; Dewey became a trustee in 1897, and his daughter was named for Jane Addams. He was for many years a frequent guest lecturer at Hull-House.

Dewey and Addams corresponded regularly and enthusiastically on pragmatism, education, and democracy, complimenting each other and acknowledging their creative interaction. When Addams showed Dewey her essay "A Modern Lear," which analyzed the violent Pullman Strike of 1894, he responded that it was one of the most insightful things he'd ever read. Dewey's letters to Addams frequently referred to their animated discussions of social psychology, the impact of which he freely acknowledged. He commented at one point that she had changed his mind on important issues and signed his letter, "Gratefully yours." After his death in 1939, his daughter wrote, "Dewey's faith in democracy as a guiding force in education took on both a sharper and a deeper meaning because of Hull-House and Jane Addams" (Farrell 1967, 69).

Addams's best writing was always fundamentally autobiographical: she could extrapolate from her own experiences, positive and negative, into a broader picture of human needs and growth. The effectiveness of this method depends, of course, on the reader's perception of the balance be-tween shared experience and irreproducible singularity of experience among human beings. Addams believed profoundly that the greater weight lay with the commonality of needs and emotions. Whether one agrees with her or not, her best prose rings with this conviction and with the deep empathy it engendered. *The Spirit of Youth and the City Streets* (1909) was her passionate analysis of the challenges and seductions facing urban young people. It resonates with an immediate, vivid sense of the young Jane Addams as lost, confused, pushed and bullied by convention, limitation, expectation. She is keenly sympathetic to young people and vastly irritated by the stupidity of social arrangements imposed on them. She blames industrialism for isolating and segregating the generations as well as the classes, for the devaluation and disintegration of community. Her tone is as close to anger as she had yet come. The book sold well and drew wide acclaim. William James wrote to Addams, "The fact is, Madam, that you are not like the rest of us, who *seek* truth and try to express it. You *inhabit* reality" (JAMSS).

Children always held a special place at Hull-House and in Addams's life. She was never a mother, but she mothered other people all her life. She loved children as individuals, but she also saw in them the hope of civilization. To Addams, human nature was essentially good and life could be joyful; children possessed that joy, and it was the task of adults to re-discover the joyful capacity within themselves through cooperation and understanding. Addams recognized adolescence as a special, transitional time in which developing personalities were vulnerable to a wide range of influences, both nurturing and damaging. She saw growing up in the city as much more stressful than her own rural youth had been. In this she ac-cepted fully the American myth, popular since Thomas Jefferson had es-poused it, that the true American character was forged in agrarian settings and that cities were morally inferior, threatening places.

In *The Spirit of Youth and the City Streets* (1909) Addams acknowledged the attraction of social and erotic instincts in young people. She recog-nized sexuality as another expression of the universal search for beauty and belonging. While it was dangerous to repress the sexual instincts to-tally, the modern city and industrial labor bombarded adolescents with too much stimulation and no impetus toward self-control. Immigrant children, struggling with assimilation and often estranged from their par-ents and traditions, were especially isolated and at risk. Addams's solu-tions were positive, not negative: to offer creative, nurturing outlets for all youth's exuberant energy, to protect them from all kinds of adult exploitation without rigid prohibitions or controls. Addams acknowledged the deadly repetitive dullness inherent in factory work, especially among children. She suggested that better working conditions, higher production standards, and a team approach would allow workers to feel some pride in their finished product. Once again, she seemed to recognize assorted symptoms while failing to identify the disease: she held true to the liberal Progressive faith that the system could be reformed and humanized from within.

Addams was at the peak of her popularity, the most famous woman in America. She was called a saint, a genius, a hero. Ida Tarbell, a famous muckraking journalist, called Addams "First Lady of the Land." She won assorted "Woman of the Year" awards repeatedly; in New York City, a reform club voted her "Most Useful American." She was a brave, innovative campaigner for women's rights, willing to travel and speak in inconvenient, out-of-the-way locations. She agreed to act in a highly melodramatic film about women's suffrage, sharing her only silver-screen appearance with leading suffragist Anna Howard Shaw. (There are no reviews extant.) In 1900 she was invited to the Paris Exposition was a juror in social economy; she judged exhibits, gave lectures, attended many others.

More serious recognition came to her as well. In 1909 alone she was elected the first woman president of the National Conference of Charities and Corrections, and she became the first women to receive an honorary degree from Yale University. At that award ceremony, a representative of Yale declared, "She has had a prophetic vision of what might be done and militant courage united with a high order of administrative, social, and political capacity in doing and getting it done" (Linn [1935] 2000, 238). Two years later she became the first head of the new National Federation of Settlements. It is worth recalling that this was years before women could actually vote.

In popular perception Addams had somehow gone directly from her earlier image of girlish innocence to the elevated, unrealistic status of an iconic mother. Her stature went beyond what she actually did, said, or wrote; she had come to symbolize the best of American democracy, a beacon of Responsibility, Compassion, and Sacrifice whose very existence somehow salved the middle-class conscience. It was far more important— and far easier—for middle- and upper-class Americans to revere Jane Addams than it was to pay careful attention to what she actually said.

Addams was almost 45 years old when she began writing her autobiography, *Twenty Years at Hull-House*, which was published in 1910. Her life at Hull-House was full, rich, and rewarding. Mary Rozet Smith was a constant, loving presence; the two had bought a cottage together near Bar Harbor, Maine, and were spending part of each summer there. Addams was in great demand as a speaker and author; she was recognized and honored across the country and beyond. She had many good reasons for the sense of optimism that permeated her new book.

Twenty Years at Hull-House, first published in November 1910, quickly went through six printings. It sold 17,000 copies in that first year alone; the total sales during her lifetime would reach 80,000, and thousands more have been sold since then. The reviews were excellent: "a book which breathes on every page the spirit of a dedicated life," raved *Sociological Review* (Davis 1973, 174). The book was translated into German, French, and Japanese, and Addams received enthusiastic letters from all over the world.

Addams's story, as she related it in *Twenty Years*, spoke to hundreds of thousands of people—especially women—around the world who had shared both her desire for a mode of moral usefulness and her despair at ever finding it. By this point in her life, Addams accepted to a large extent the role in which her public had cast her: the gentle, brave, self-examining model of ethical womanhood. The early chapters of *Twenty Years* offer an idealized image of a small-town American childhood with the child Jane, already serious, introspective, and self-critical, aware at a young age of the rocky road ahead of her. This small-town democracy was widely remembered as the true source of all that was best in America: community *and* individualism, tradition *and* innovation, sharing and cooperation that still left room for happy entrepreneurship and proper economic rewards.

Addams frequently taps into the popular veneration for Abraham Lincoln; she doesn't hesitate to equip her costume in the American Drama with elements from Lincoln's costume. She plays up her father's relationship with Lincoln, and herself as heir to that understanding. Subtly she suggests many parallels between her life and Lincoln's: they were both from frontier Illinois, both developed reputations for lonely honesty and incorruptibility, both shouldered huge burdens and worked selflessly for others.

Twenty Years at Hull-House is also a classic American folk myth of the struggle to overcome obstacles in the search for the meaningful, admirable self. Addams makes her early back problems loom like a deformity in her early life. She uses ugly duckling imagery about herself, portraying herself as desperate for her father's approval but unworthy of it. As has been noted earlier, her father becomes a mythic figure of saintly dimensions. She does not mention her stepmother at all. It is true that theirs was a difficult, contentious relationship, but Anna Huy Haldeman had been a real presence in Jane Addams's life for almost 40 years, and she still was very much so when *Twenty Years* was written. Her total absence from the book says a great deal about the kind of past Addams wanted to offer her readers, and how carefully she controlled it.

Twenty Years at Hull-House was written for higher purposes than straightforward autobiographical accuracy (to whatever extent such a thing is possible). The first half of the book takes young Jane through childhood, recounts her searching and questioning at Rockford, takes her through the lost years of travel, loneliness, and confusion. To lend significance to her stories, to make sure that the reader can't miss the moral signposts along the way, Addams frequently revised her memories of past events. She gives a vivid depiction of an intercollegiate oratorical contest during her senior year at Rockford. She sadly lost, she writes, to a young man from Illinois College named William Jennings Bryan, who went on to be a famous lawyer, speaker, and presidential candidate; how could she have triumphed over such future greatness? The problem is that the event Addams describes never took place. Addams had come to the competition with the girls from Rockford, but as an observer, not a contestant; and Bryant had actually lost an earlier round and was not competing at the high level Addams witnessed.

Again, in her chapter on the lost years Addams emphasizes her depression and insecurity and makes much of a trip into the slums of East London as a harbinger of her plan to found Hull-House. The climax of the chapter is a scene at a bullfight in Spain, where Addams reacts with mixed disgust and fascination to the brutal violence. Her horror at her own attraction to the spectacle is somehow cast a transformative moment, in which she perceives the emptiness of further observing other cultures and other lives and resolves to go home and *do something*. That something, she tells Ellen Starr the next day, will become Hull-House. But neither Addams's contemporaneous journals of the trip nor her letters home reveal any such profound moral insight or decisiveness. This is active myth making. This is within the long tradition of spiritual autobiography, in which the wandering narrator recalls the Conversion Experience that showed her/him the Way. Years later Addams admitted to her beloved nephew and biographer that specific dates were difficult for her to remember and that she had been deliberately vague about such things. "Well, they do not seem very important in my life. It has just flowed on. And besides, if I don't give dates, I can't be wrong about them" (Linn [1935] 2000, 256).

The second half of *Twenty Years* focuses on Hull-House itself. Addams presents the magnificent solution to all her earlier problems, and Hull-House takes over as the dominant personality. Addams retreats from the intimacy she had offered readers earlier; she is less personal now, she has found her way to Hull-House and has no more room for self-doubt or false starts. She is busy, eager, and fulfilled even while modeling the best in American modesty. These latter chapters are a hymn to progress, to her optimistic perspective on the human community and its capacity for connectedness. She even describes her joining a church as an expression of egalitarianism, a step into universal fellowship. Taken as a whole the book follows an earnest, well-intentioned young woman through the perils of a privileged but unfocused youth until she finds meaning in her own life through service to others at Hull-House. The real faith is that all human problems can be solved if people of goodwill apply themselves with compassion, understanding, and good old American hard work.

Perhaps the height of Addams's national political involvement was her work with the Progressive Party. At the Republican national convention in Chicago in June of 1912, a triangular power war developed among Robert La Follette; William Howard Taft, the incumbent; and Theodore Roosevelt, who had been President William McKinley's vice president, had come to the presidency as a result of McKinley's assassination in 1901, and had been elected himself in 1904. Roosevelt was brilliant, charismatic, and the favorite of most rank and file delegates, but the party bosses were with Taft, and they controlled the formal mechanics of awarding delegate seats. When Roosevelt recognized the full extent of Taft's advantage, he ordered his own delegates to withdraw from the convention. Taft won the Republican nomination easily, and Roosevelt's supporters began organizing a new party.

The new Progressive Party convened in Chicago on August 5th with wild enthusiasm and great hopes. The party platform included tariff reform, stricter regulation of big business, minimum wage standards, and women's suffrage. Roosevelt seemed to embody all the vibrant energy and optimism of the Progressive Era, as did Jane Addams. Initially, Roosevelt had little use for Addams. He was irritated and skeptical of the saintly image the popular media offered of Addams; he thought her too sentimental and considered Tolstoy's influence on her as inappropriate for America. He once called her "poor bleeding Jane" and referred to her as a "progressive mouse" (Phillips 1974, 50). But his needs as a maverick candidate changed his public perceptions of this most highly regarded woman.

Addams herself, ever practical and concrete in her goals, looked beyond Teddy Roosevelt's posturing and saw a reform platform that would
address many of the major inequities in America. She had come increasingly to recognize the need for national standards to protect the poor and
working class, especially women and children. Just that year Taft had appointed Hull-House family member Julia Lathrop to head the new national Children's Bureau. Roosevelt assured Addams that he was
unequivocally in favor of women's suffrage, and Addams, a gifted compro-
miser, became a highly visible, influential supporter.

The compromises were substantial, however. Addams had already
moved to a deeply pacifist, internationalist stance, while Roosevelt was a
gleeful militarist who saw combat as the ultimate expression of masculinity. More immediately, Roosevelt courted wavering Southern progressives
by pandering to their racism: although there were African American delegates from a number of northern states, Roosevelt refused to seat any
from Southern states. Addams, standing in the shadows of Abraham Lincoln and her beloved abolitionist father, was appalled. She argued for the
inclusion of Southern black delegates to no avail. She accepted defeat and
maintained her outspoken support for the Party, much to the disappointment of many of her friends.

In truth, there was no good choice to make in American politics over
the issue of racism. Since Reconstruction after the Civil War, the Republican Party had been despised in the South; Addams could see no hope of
any real effort to address race within the party. The Democratic candidate, Woodrow Wilson, had grown up in a slave-owning family in Virginia and held deeply racist attitudes. (As President, Wilson would
segregate the Civil Service, treat the new NAACP with open contempt,
and call the profoundly racist film *Birth of a Nation* the greatest film ever
made.)

Nonetheless, Roosevelt did at least articulate a program that addressed
the manifold woes of industrial America. Addams was genuinely excited
by the party platform, which had been hammered out in consultation
with the National Conference of Charities and Correction and included
vast improvements in safety standards, hours, child labor, and housing.
She believed that the Progressive program had the potential to foster an
atmosphere of increasing tolerance and mutual understanding—her ultimate goal. The platform even called for a federal program to provide accident, old age, and unemployment insurance.

Addams was also, no doubt, flattered by the massive publicity focused
on her when she seconded Roosevelt's nomination at the convention.

Her speech on that occasion focused on America's shocking, shabby treatment of its workforce. She pointed out that 29 European countries forbade all nighttime factory work by women, while only 3 states in America did so. Her data indicated that 15,000 men were killed annually in mining and factory accidents; 500,000 were severely injured or crippled. It was as if every adult male in the state of Maine were maimed each year. Addams tapped into Roosevelt's militarism when she declared that unregulated industrialism was a battlefield and its victims were war casualties; in effect, she was demanding that responsible government fight back to protect its workers.

Addams was a star attraction and a dedicated campaigner once she had committed herself. She toured the entire country speaking for Roosevelt, from Los Angeles to North Dakota to Worcester, Massachusetts. Everywhere she was met by cheering throngs. A Jane Addams Songbook was published, and choruses of young women would perform from it at her rallies. She was an effective fundraiser, although her entry into formal politics complicated her carefully constructed nonpartisan image. Racial reformers were critical of her compromise, however reluctant, on the seating of black delegates at the convention; peace activists decried her associating herself with Roosevelt's boisterous militarism and imperialism.

In the end, her efforts were wasted. Roosevelt lost the election to Woodrow Wilson, and an embittered Roosevelt began to swing to the right to regain his prestige in the Republican Party. He was looking toward the 1916 presidential election, and he wanted funds for an extravagant campaign; he courted Big Business with increasingly conservative, anti-reform positions. Without his driving personality and commitment, the Progressive Party began to fragment. Disillusioned, Addams distanced herself from the entire process of national politics until the outbreak of the catastrophic Great War in 1914. For the rest of her life, she was consumed by a dedication to pacifism that overrode and underlay all her other concerns.

Jane Addams, 1868. Courtesy of University of Illinois at Chicago, University Library, Department of Special Collections, Jane Addams Memorial Collection, JAMC neg. 2.

Businessman and state senator, John Huy Addams, Jane's father. Courtesy of University of Illinois at Chicago, University Library, Department of Special Collections, Jane Addams Memorial Collection, JAMC neg. 622.

Jane Addams, Anna Haldeman Addams, and George Haldeman, 1876. Courtesy of University of Illinois at Chicago, University Library, Department of Special Collections, Jane Addams Memorial Collection, JAMC neg. 42.

Hull-House, 1891–1894, as it would have looked when Jane Addams first moved in. Courtesy of University of Illinois at Chicago, University Library, Department of Special Collections, Jane Addams Memorial Collection, JAMC neg. 146.

Jane Addams and friends in her Hull-House apartment, circa 1889. Courtesy of University of Illinois at Chicago, University Library, Department of Special Collections, Jane Addams Memorial Collection, JAMC neg. 992.

Ellen Gates Starr, circa 1889. Courtesy of University of Illinois at Chicago, University Library, Department of Special Collections, Jane Addams Memorial Collection, JAMC neg. 428.

Right: Jane Addams and Bishop George Vincent at Chatauqua, New York, circa 1910. Courtesy of University of Illinois at Chicago, University Library, Department of Special Collections, Jane Addams Memorial Collection, JAMC neg. 49.

Below: Jane Addams with suffragists and Bull Moose supporters, 1912. From left to right, back row, Margaret D. Robins, Women's Trade Union League; Jane Addams, Louise deKoven Bowen, Treasurer of Hull-House Association; and (seated), Mary J. Hawes Willmarth, Hull-House trustee and president of the Woman's City Club of Chicago, and Edith Wyatt, novelist, journalist, and social activist. Courtesy of University of Illinois at Chicago, University Library, Department of Special Collections, Jane Addams Memorial Collection, JAMC neg. 1235.

Above: Jane Addams on her world tour, 1922–1923, in Osaka, Japan. Courtesy of University of Illinois at Chicago, University Library, Department of Special Collections, Jane Addams Memorial Collection, JAMC neg. 60.

Left: Jane Addams and Mary Rozet Smith, 1930. Courtesy of University of Illinois at Chicago, University Library, Department of Special Collections, Jane Addams Memorial Collection, JAMC neg. 592.

One of the last photographs taken of Jane Addams, Hull-House courtyard, 1935. Courtesy of University of Illinois at Chicago, University Library, Department of Special Collections, Jane Addams Memorial Collection, JAMC neg. 1228.

Chapter 6

PEACE AND WAR

The Victorian worldview depicted women as generally inferior to men—less intelligent, physically weaker, unable to withstand the rigors of the competitive working world, too sensitive to be exposed to the many evils and problems of real life. Despite manifest evidence to the contrary, there is little doubt that most men believed the myth—or at least found it convenient to act as though they did. Many women, brought up on the dogma, believed parts of it—or at least found it easier to accept their restricted lives if they pretended they did.

The only superiority women were encouraged to assume was moral. The *Wife and Mother*, succoring her tired husband and raising proper, clean, Christian children, was the ideal. The image was a useful one, adaptable to a variety of reform agendas. Even bold, imaginative women busy demanding nontraditional rights kept the cloak of Motherhood wrapped tightly about themselves. Many of the women organizing for causes were too sophisticated to take this pious role literally, but it was a powerful rhetorical tool and they used it well. Similarly, the image of men as more prone to violence, greed, and cruelty provided ammunition for crusading women.

Women led the fight for temperance—abstinence from or minimal use of alcoholic beverages—because they believed that its alternative was intemperance. That thread of intemperance snaked from the private horrors of domestic violence to local brawls and crime and out into the monstrous wars of history. Mothers were perceived as the guardians of Life, the natural opponents of violence in all its manifestations. Susan B. Anthony and Elizabeth Cady Stanton, the most prominent of women's rights advocates, founded the New York State Women's Temperance Society in 1852, only four years after their historic conference on women's rights in Seneca Falls.

The national Woman's Christian Temperance Union (WCTU) was founded by Frances Willard in 1874; Willard viewed peace as a primary woman's issue because she saw alcohol abuse as inextricably linked to militarism, the organized expression of violence. By the 1890s the WCTU was by far the largest, most influential women's organization in the United States, with over 150,000 members. A Quaker member of the WCTU, Hannah Bailey, who had experience within several existing organizations that promoted nonviolence, initiated the WCTU's Department of Peace and Arbitration in 1887. The idea of a women's peace organization represented potent intersection of religion, peace, and voting rights and allowed women to combine activism with domesticity. This section of the WCTU attracted thousands of members around the world; it lobbied Congress and it published two monthly journals, one for adults and one for children, that argued against military expenditure, lynching, military training in schools, conscription, and violent sports. They even recognized the insidious role of war toys in encouraging violent play in boys.

In the United States, the special context was the shared anguish and losses of the Civil War barely 20 years before, with its staggering 618,000 deaths. There was a sense among many women that some of the basic characteristics by which men defined and valued themselves were not particularly good for society. Peace-minded women argued that patriotism was not grounded in war. They distrusted the materialistic greed of imperialism; they feared—justifiably—that soldiers could come home from wars in exotic places to spread venereal disease in their own homes. In 1895, Lillie Devereux Blake, a leading New York suffragist, told an audience that men were willing to "deluge the world in blood for a strip of land in Venezuela or a gold mine in Africa" (EGSP, Sophia Smith Collection).

By the 1890s the entire global power structure was being reconfigured by rapidly growing new technologies and the supply/raw materials demands they generated. New metals called for reliable ore sources; both military and commercial steam shipping depended on refueling at island coal stations. On February 15, 1898, the United States entered the imperial game quite literally explosively when the battleship *Maine* blew up in the harbor of Havana, Cuba, with the loss of 260 lives. Cuba, then a possession of Spain, had already endured a previous 10-year insurrection (1868–1878), and American sugar and shipping interests had been actively aiding the new rebellion that had begun in 1895. No reliable explanation for the *Maine's* destruction was ever discovered, but the well-orchestrated propaganda campaigns of many sensationalist newspapers in the United States whipped public opinion into a righteous war frenzy. Spain quickly agreed to submit to American mediation of its dispute with Cuba, but it was a "splendid little war," not dull, protracted negotiations, that American business and political leadership wanted. By the end of April the United States and Spain were officially at war. Ten weeks later, American forces had destroyed the Spanish fleet in both Cuba and the Philippine Islands (another Spanish colony), and taken control of the resource-rich islands as well as Puerto Rico in the Caribbean and Guam in the Pacific. The United States had become an imperial power.

Suddenly, the old American assumptions of isolationism, of the United States as somehow separate from the rest of the world, were profoundly challenged. While the mainstream press celebrated the new acquisitions, many thoughtful people were appalled at the image of American troops suppressing nationalist liberation movements in both Cuba and the Philippines. In June 1898 the Anti-Imperialist League was founded in Boston by leading men, writer Mark Twain and steel tycoon Andrew Carnegie among them, who represented a broad spectrum of political and cultural positions. Women's groups had been particularly angered at the treatment of the Filipinos and at images of drunkenness and prostitution rampant on the new overseas military bases; groups like the National Council of Women, the WCTU, and the National American Woman Suffrage Association all spoke out against the occupation of the Philippines. Jane Addams and many other suffragists supported the Anti-Imperialist League, although women were not permitted to serve as officers until 1904.

As a child and a young woman, Jane Addams had had no special reason to be aware of violence as an issue in human affairs. Nor had her father been in any way a pacifist. She respected Tolstoy and the choices he had made, but she could not accept them for herself; quite the contrary: while Tolstoy, as a radical Christian, rejected the state altogether, Addams increasingly placed her greatest hopes in the potential of a humane state that would elicit the best of human behavior.

The Spanish-American War drew Addams to anti-imperialism and peace advocacy. She could see the impact of the war mentality in the rising street violence and increasingly brutal games among the children in her neighborhood; it was in her eyes as though the fog of unleashed militarism clouded the entire human landscape and prevented people from recognizing each other's basic humanity. Addams helped found the

Chicago branch of the Anti-Imperialist League and in 1899 made an impassioned public speech in which she denounced flag-waving patriotism that had been divorced from any sense of civic responsibility or community. She argued for the first time that society needed to adapt the courage and selflessness of the war-time experience to its urgent peace-time crises. With a timeless understanding, she wrote, "The great pity of it all is that war tends to fix our minds on the picturesque, that it seems so much more magnificent to do battle for the right than patiently to correct the wrong" (Davis 1973, 142).

Peace, she declared, was "no longer merely absence of war, but the unfolding of life processes which are making for a common development" (Fisher 2004, 74). By "common" Addams meant a sense of shared humanity that utterly transcended national identities. "Unless the present situation extends our nationalism into internationalism, unless it has thrust forward our patriotism into humanitarianism, we cannot meet it...National events determine our ideals, as much as our ideals determine national events" (Addams 1899, 3).

In the spring of 1903 Addams gave a speech at the Ethical Culture Society in which she called for "a moral substitute for war." The following autumn she expanded the idea in an address to the Universal Peace Conference in Boston, declaring, "The thing that is incumbent on this generation is to discover a moral substitute for war, something that will appeal to the courage, the capacity of men, something which will develop their finest powers without deteriorating their moral natures, as war constantly does" (Schott 1993, 247). She urged the formation of an international welfare community, arguing that the labor and social reform movements provided peaceful examples of the communal ideals of service and trust so valued in the camaraderie of war. (This interpretation of public service would eventually bear fruit in the Civilian Conservation Corps of the Depression era and in the Peace Corps.) The pragmatist philosopher William James shared the podium with Addams in 1904, and he was inspired by her vision of fulfillment through service; he had already been searching for ways to tap into the positive energies and experiences of heroism and sacrifice without the hideous costs of war. James's much more well-known essay, "The Moral Equivalent of War," was not published until 1910.

Addams developed these ideas further in *Newer Ideals of Peace*, published in 1907. As she described it, the American Revolution had been a revolt of the privileged to protect their own advantages, tainted with militaristic attitudes. "[O]ur early democracy was a moral romanticism, rather than a well-grounded belief in social capacity and in the efficiency of the popular will" (Fisher 2004, 78). Addams described an American society and economy that ran on exploitation and selfishness beneath the illusion of rights. She declared that the entire concept of government needed to change to meet the new challenges posed by intense immigration and crowded cities. She saw polyglot, multicultural neighborhoods like Hull-House's as incubators for greater awareness and recognition of shared humanity; it was logical to extrapolate from that model into an ideal of mixed nations. Similarly, she moved from the specific image of the nurturing mother within a family to the declaration that all women had a special interest in peace and an active responsibility for fostering nonviolent attitudes.

The early twentieth century was a turbulent moment for peace advocates. The Russo-Japanese of 1904–1905, fought over economic interests in Manchuria, was the first war among the major powers in 35 years, the first war fought with the newly developed machine guns and rapid-fire artillery. Casualties were massive; the world was appalled, and peace societies felt a surge in membership. In the 10 years before the outbreak of the First World War, the U.S. State Department was dominated by men who had been officers in various peace groups; both Presidents William Taft and Woodrow Wilson supported the concept of international peace. In the spirit of the moment, Boston publisher Edward Ginn started the World Peace Fund in 1910 with an initial grant of $1,000,000. The following year Andrew Carnegie, king of the steel industry, established the Carnegie Endowment for International Peace with 10 million dollars. Hope ran high throughout the movement. The new membership included lawyers, businessmen, economists, and educators. They were not naïve idealists; they were searching for common ground, international tools for conflict resolution, establishment of a level of international law, a world court to administer it and an international police force to enforce it.

Women were a major force in this vitalized peace movement. The year 1899 saw the first World Peace Conference at The Hague in the Netherlands. A broad range of women's groups took part in the Hague conference and went on to the first general gathering of the International Council of Women in London that same year. The Council had been founded 11 years earlier in Washington, D.C. as an international women's suffrage organization. It quickly expanded its mission to embrace issues of peace, war, and domestic violence, arguing that women were naturally more pacific than men and that women would vote for nonviolent solutions. Much of the thoughtful focus was on military training in schools; anticipating later developments in social and educational psychology, the women argued that boys should be socialized away from militarism and toward more responsible, caring behavior. They confronted head-on profound questions of what constituted basic masculinity—and whether the modern world could survive on primitive definitions. As noted economist and author Charlotte Perkins Gillman wrote in *Our Man Made World* in 1911, "in warfare, *per se*, we find maleness in its absurdist extremes. Here is…the whole gamut of basic masculinity, from the initial instinct of combat, through every glorious form of ostentation with the loudest possible accompaniment of noise" (Alonso 1993, 61). By the early twentieth century the International Council of Women and the new International Alliance of Women represented over 6,000,000 female members around the world. They corresponded with each other, worked on committees together, conducted sophisticated research and analysis, organized large annual meetings at which they were energized, reassured, and inspired by each other's commitment. The foundation for the Woman's Peace Party (WPP) was well laid before the Great War broke out.

In the first decade of the twentieth century the balance of power in Europe teetered precariously between two alliances: the Triple Alliance, or Central Powers (Germany, Austria-Hungary, and Italy), and the Triple Entente (England, France, and Russia). The technology of armaments was advancing rapidly, and most of these countries responded with massive expansions of their armed forces, especially navies. Antagonism and tension were already high when, in late June of 1914, a Serbian revolutionary assassinated the heir to the Austro-Hungarian throne, Archduke Franz Ferdinand. Austria declared war on Serbia one month later; Russia mobilized her army to defend Slavic interests; further declarations of war ricocheted around Europe, and by August the first global war had begun.

The scale of this war was unlike anything the world had ever seen. The destruction and losses were almost incomprehensible; with no real causes and no articulated goals, the war spread like an uncontrollable wildfire across Europe, trapping troops and civilians alike in its path. President Wilson formally declared American neutrality in September. There was almost universal relief among Americans that the United States was not directly involved in the conflict, although historically and culturally, most Americans could sympathize more readily with England and France than with Germany and Austria-Hungary. The popular press demonized Germany, and public sentiment against all things Teutonic lurched toward hysteria.

Public patriotism and government censorship combined to stifle dissent with unusual ferocity. Nonetheless, there already existed a large group of peace advocates who were highly educated; expert in relevant fields like economics, law, political science, and social psychology; and experienced in international organizing. From the early days of the war, Jane Addams argued for an international conference of experts to frame mediation initiatives with the belligerent nations; in her plan, these experts would speak for all humanity rather than on behalf of specific governments, which were all compromised by their own agendas. Peace activists recognized that public opinion, even the enlightened public opinion they sought to elicit, would not be sufficient in itself to establish and maintain world peace. By January 1915 a group of prominent Americans, among them former President William Howard Taft, founded the Association for a League to Enforce Peace. This new association seemed daring to many, but it was careful to emphasize postwar plans and it consistently refused to address any proposals to end the current war by mediation and compromise.

To the women most urgently involved in the peace movement, this was utterly unacceptable, much too little much too late. With many other sophisticated opponents of the war, they were also acutely aware of the profound ways in which the new scale and production of war were changing the country. Despite official neutrality, American banking and heavy industry became quickly and deeply invested in the Triple Entente cause. As early as September 1914, John Haynes Homes, a leading Unitarian minister, published an article in *The Survey* exhorting peace activists to join forces against the root causes of war: "first, militarism; second, political autocracy; and third, commercialism. The axe must be laid at the roots of the tree—which are armaments, dynasties, and exploitation" (Chambers 1991, 41). By the spring of 1915, Bethlehem Steel alone held over 100 million dollars in contracts from Great Britain for shell casings and shrapnel; the banking/investment house of J.P. Morgan opened a special "Purchasing Bureau" to handle all the war-related business that poured in. Contemporaneous historian Walter Millis described how "New York hotels were swarming with eager competitors for the unparalleled profits of death," and he commented bluntly on "the new militarist-imperialist industrialism rapidly developing in the United States" (Millis 1935, 197, 199).

To Addams, war represented the ultimate obstacle in the struggle to expand human understanding and tolerance. From the outbreak of the First World War, world peace became her major commitment; she devoted most of her energies and time to organizing, speaking, world travel, refugee problems and famine relief. Her efforts were direct, anguished, and passionate, but she never surrendered the methodical discipline that made her such a respected adversary. James Linn recalled, "[I]t was a struggled based not on emotion, and not on economic principles, but on understanding. It was a fight for comprehension" (Linn [1935] 2000, 285). Under the potent leadership of Addams, the WPP maintained a consistent, logical anti-imperialist position. It protested the United States military occupation of Haiti in 1915, criticizing especially a United States-imposed treaty that granted American sweeping controls over Haiti's business and finances for 20 years. In addition, the WPP protested the expenditure of $3,000,000 for American bases in Nicaragua; it protested against United States troops in the Dominican Republic and Nicaragua, against corrupt colonial governments in Puerto Rico and the Philippines, and against the United States purchase of the Virgin Islands from Denmark without a vote among the islanders themselves.

Addams and thousands of other women saw only too clearly how the war would derail the campaign for women's rights; they readily acknowledged that as women they had a special role in the peace movement. The first public American protest against the war was a parade organized by leading women's rights activists in New York City on August 29, 1914, less than a month into the war. Over 1,500 women dressed in mourning marched in silence to the beat of muffled drums. The march signaled an impatience with the male-dominated major peace organizations, a determination to bring a separate female voice to the antiwar movement. The next month Addams chaired a peace conference at the Henry Street Settlement in New York. As she reported, "It was in the early fall of 1914 that a small group of social workers held the first of a series of meetings at the Henry Street Settlement in New York, trying to formulate the reaction to war on the part of those who for many years had devoted their energies to the reduction of devastating poverty" (Addams [1922–1945] 1960, 3).

That same month Rosika Schwimmer, a Hungarian journalist and suffragist, arrived in New York, carrying a large petition she had circulated among European women asking Woodrow Wilson to lead a mediating board of neutral nations. Her petition was signed by over 200,000 women from 13 countries. Accompanied by Carrie Chapmann Catt, an officer of the International Woman's Suffrage Alliance, Schwimmer met with both President Wilson and Secretary of State William Jennings Bryan; the women were treated with genteel dismissiveness.

The Woman's Peace Party grew directly from the speaking tour of Rosika Schwimmer and Emmeline Pethick-Lawrence, an English suffragist and pacifist who had been imprisoned in England for her suffrage protests. Pethick-Lawrence urged American women to unite as never before for suffrage as an instrument of peace. It was essential to the survival of the human race, she wrote, that "the mother half of humanity should now be admitted to articulate citizenship" (Farrell 1967, 150 fn24). As Chapman Catt, a leading suffragist, wrote angrily to Addams about the male leadership of the major peace organizations, "It would seem that they have as little use for women and their points of view as have the militarists" (Woman's Peace Party Papers, SCPC). In New York City Pethick-Lawrence and Schwimmer met with Madeline Zabrisky Doty, a radical lawyer committed to coordinating suffrage activities with the new campaign for peace mediation. Doty's friend, socialist lawyer Crystal Eastman, brought in the militant Women's Political Union, led by Harriot Stanton Blatch, daughter of Elizabeth Cady Stanton. These women established the first Woman's Peace Party, even while they acknowledged that as a group they were seen as too radical and bohemian to have national appeal. They needed older, more mainstream figures for the national movement.

Catt proposed to Addams that the two of them issue a call to women's organizations for a national conference in Washington to focus on peace efforts. In actuality, Catt was concerned that too much prominence in the peace movement might jeopardize her suffragist leadership, and she gladly stepped back to leave Addams in the role of conference organizer. At the same time, Addams worked with Lillian Wald of Henry Street Settlement; Paul Kellogg, editor of *The Survey*; Roger Baldwin, who would go on to found the American Civil Liberties Union; and other peace activists to form the American League for the Limitation of Armaments, which soon changed its name to the American Union Against Militarism (AUAM). This group lobbied intensively, mounted major letter-writing campaigns, and managed to prevent the passage of a bill mandating military training in nation-wide public high school physical education programs. The New York branch of the WPP organized an art exhibit entitled "War Against War," which drew 6,000 to 8,000 spectators each day and moved from Brooklyn to Manhattan, Boston, and Chicago.

Initially, Addams was reluctant to establish a separate women's peace organization; it seemed somehow a capitulation to sexual inequality. But the urging of many women, combined with the intransigence of the men in the American Peace Society and the rapidly expanding horrors of the war, soon convinced her. In response to Addams's call, over 3,000 women gathered in Washington and declared the formation of the national Woman's Peace Party on January 10, 1915. Addams chaired the meeting

and was overwhelmingly elected the first president. The delegates came
from the intensely conservative Daughters of the American Revolution;
the Women's Christian Temperance Union; the militantly suffragist Congressional Union; the Women's Trade Union League; the Women's National Committee of the Socialist Party. They represented a wide
ideological range on many issues, but they were united in the belief that
full rights for women were utterly central to a true peace grounded in justice and stability. In an impassioned speech to the gathering entitled
"What War is Destroying," Addams addressed the historical and cultural
roles of women as bearers, nurturers, and healers of life. "I do not assert
that women are better than men—even in the heat of suffrage debates I
have never maintained that—but we would all admit that there are things
concerning which women are more sensitive than men, and that one of
these is the treasuring of life" (Fischer 2004, 87).

To the WPP, this special awareness carried with it an enormous responsibility. The platform of the group focused on immediate neutral mediation to end the current conflict, on arms limitation, democratic
control of foreign policy, creation of international laws and an international police force instead of national armies; and specific programs of aid
and regulation to eliminate the causes of this and future wars. Above all,
the platform demanded that women throughout the world have a full
voice in the policies and decisions that could shatter their lives and loved
ones: "Therefore, as human beings and the mother half of humanity, we
demand that our right to be consulted in the settlement of questions concerning not alone the life of individuals but of nations be recognized and
respected. We demand that women be given a share in deciding between
war and peace in all courts of high debate—within the home, the school,
the church, the industrial order, and the state" (Chambers 1991, 51).

In these meetings Addams articulated eloquently a position on the full
impact and costs of war that she would maintain consistently for the rest
of her life. She had worked so hard to define a positive role for the state in
nurturing, protecting, and enriching human life—all functions she knew
would be lost and corrupted in war. War itself, and the emotions it exacerbated, would destroy the hope for any advance in compassion and moral
growth. "We know," she admonished sadly, "that Europe at the end of this
war will not begin to build where it left off; we know that it will begin generations behind the point it had reached when the war began" (Chambers
1991, 55).

The Woman's Peace Party grew at an astonishing rate. There were 85
charter members at that first meeting in 1915; by the end of that year

there were over 30 local branches throughout the country. Membership peaked at 40,000 early in 1916. America's entry into the war on April 6, 1917, would complicate pacifist appeals and result in a sharp drop in participation. But the dedicated activist core, watching helplessly as Europe seemed bound for total self-destruction that first hideous winter, determined that like-minded women throughout the world had to take some sort of international action, to raise a voice of reason in a world gone mad. Despite enormous difficulties with censorship, communication in wartime, unofficial repercussions, fear, hatred, and more mundane logistics, the seeds had been planted that would grow into the International Congress of Women held at The Hague, the Netherlands, in May 1915.

Chapter 7

THE HOPES OF THE HAGUE

There was no way that the people of Europe could have anticipated the horrors of this new war. By the end of 1914 millions of men faced each other across an artificial front of trenches extending over 475 miles from the North Sea to the Alps. Life in the trenches was an unrelieved horror. The men lived with the constant threat of death from the random fire of snipers. It was never safe to leave the trenches, and personal hygiene and sanitation were impossible. Bodily functions were performed in the trench, with waste removal haphazard and unreliable. The trenches frequently flooded, leaving the soldiers standing day and night up to their knees or even their waists in bloody, contaminated water. Rats swam freely about, feasting on the unburied corpses of casualties; the rat infestation was so severe that most regiments traveled with portable kennels for their rat terriers. "Lice, rats, barbed wire, fleas, shells, bombs, underground caves, corpses, blood, liquor, mice, cats, artillery, filth, bullets, mortars, fire, steel," wrote the German expressionist artist Otto Dix about trench warfare. "It is the work of the devil" (Berson 1999, 55). The Gallipoli campaign in Turkey was a hideous disaster, in which Australian troops were driven into suicidal confrontations with larger Turkish forces. All of this festered amidst widening reports of Turkish genocide against the civilian Armenian populace; a massive 1,800-mile front with Russia was the site of frequent bloody, pointless battles. No one could claim any realistic intentions or design for the conduct of this lurching catastrophe, but each new assault or atrocity on any side served to lock the respective governments more tightly into ill-thought, unimaginative, reactive positions.

In this poisoned atmosphere, Addams and other women called for an international gathering of mediation minded individuals who would speak for all humanity, beyond the limited voices and vested interests of particular governments. In February 1915 Addams received a cable from Dr. Aletta Jacobs, the Dutch leader of a group of European feminists, urging her to preside at an international peace meeting. There had been a meeting of the International Woman Suffrage Alliance scheduled for Berlin that spring, which the war had derailed. With great difficulty, small groups of British, German, Dutch, Italian, Hungarian, Swiss, French, and Belgian organizers were able to meet in Amsterdam and redesign the suffrage meeting as an antiwar gathering set in The Hague in the neutral Netherlands.

It took incredible determination and courage among these women: nowhere did they have the vote, and everywhere they were subjected to vicious attack and vilification from prowar elements and the press. Even in ostensibly neutral United States, former President Theodore Roosevelt contemptuously called them "hysterical pacifists" (Chambers 1991, 2). In the words of Mary Chamberlain, a reporter for *The Survey* who attended the conference, "It was a great test of courage for these women to risk the bitterness of their families, the ridicule of their friends and the censure of their governments to come to this international woman's congress" (Chamberlain 1915, 220).

Deliberate obstacles were thrown in their path. The five Belgian delegates, whose country was under German occupation, had to apply for special permission from German authorities to attend the meeting. They traveled by car as far as Eschen, where they were stopped and searched, and their car was confiscated. They struggled on foot for over two hours to Rosendahl inside Holland, where they were able to find a train to The Hague. One hundred eighty British women accepted invitations to the conference, but only two actually arrived on time. The other 178 found their numbers reduced to 24 for no legitimate reason by the Secretary of Foreign Affairs, who advised the Home Office to limit the number of passports issued. Officials claimed that so large a group of Englishwomen so near the front would represent a danger to the security of the nation; they might somehow fall prey to German spies. Even the surviving 24 were disingenuously delayed at Folkestone in Kent, waiting for a boat to get them to Holland. With no real explanation, the British government suddenly suspended all travel between England and Holland, effectively stranding the British delegation. On April 16 the American delegation, 47 strong led by Jane Addams, sailed from New York on the Dutch ship

Noordam. The conference was almost sabotaged again when the British inexplicably delayed the ship at Folkestone for three days, but it was finally released to complete its voyage.

In all, 1,136 delegates from 12 countries met that April in The Hague, despite much official and unofficial opposition. Very few British women made it through the shabby British obstacle course, and none was able to come from Russia or France. Women attended from Sweden, Norway, Italy, Hungary, Germany, Denmark, Canada, Belgium, Austria, Great Britain, the Netherlands, and the United States. Most of these women were experienced organizers and analyzers, willing to withstand the anger and hostility of their own neighbors and countrymen. The German delegates included founders of the woman's suffrage movement in Germany as well as leaders in the workers' rights movement and in the League for the Protection of Mothers and the League for the Care of Prisoners. The war was barely 8 months old, raging mercilessly around them and killing literally thousands of young men every day. These educated, experienced women gathered together at such great effort because they believed that only a strong mediating voice from the neutral nations could spare the world further years of anguish. They refused to believe that the hideous momentum established by daily brutality and fear could not be deflected by reason and compassion. The German and English delegates sat side by side, and German women shook hands with Belgians.

Jane Addams was elected the first president of the International Congress of Women for Permanent Peace. Despite the unity of purpose they all felt, no one doubted the magnitude of the task before them. They were looking for profound social change, which they believed alone would lead toward the elimination of injustice and the simmering resentments that could so easily be manipulated into misguided patriotic rage. As Addams wrote in the opening notes of the program, they were convinced "that one of the strongest forces for the prevention of war will be the combined influence of the women of all countries.... But as women can only make their influence effective if they have equal political rights with men, this Congress declares that it is the duty of the women of all countries to work with all their force for their political enfranchisement" (WPPP).

The mood of the conference was one of urgency and grief. "Everybody talks about victory," Rosika Schwimmer commented, "but we women know that every victory means the death of thousands of sons of other mothers" (Chamberlain 1915, 222). The convention worked out a series of proposals involving nonstop mediation sessions chaired by the neutral powers, an ongoing process designed to break through the competitive fears that so dominated and undermined the diplomatic landscape. They hoped for something positive that might be salvaged out of the wreckage of Europe: "a new birth of internationalism, founded not so much upon arbitration treaties, to be used in time of disturbance, as upon governmental devices designed to protect and enhance fruitful processes of cooperation in the great experiment of living together in a world become conscious of itself" (Addams et al. 1915, 141).

Addams had tremendous faith in the potential goodness of government; as the direct expression of society the state could be an entity that expressed the combined values of the people—which, for Addams, included sharing and cooperation even more deeply than aggression. The differences among groups, in her vision, were far less significant than the shared needs and hopes. She believed that reason could defuse emotionalism. She wrote of the need for objectivity: "We came to feel that what is needed above all else is some human interpretation of this overevolved and much-talked-of situation in which so much of the world finds itself in dire confusion and bloodshed" (Addams et al. 1915, 56).

Throughout the summer of 1915 several delegations of women from The Hague conference traveled across Europe presenting their mediation proposals to foreign ministers and prime ministers. "Our mission was simple," Addams reported, "and foolish it may be, but it was not impossible" (Addams et al. 1915, 97). They hoped to help end the war, but the hope, however fervent, was always fragile. Even Alice Hamilton, Addams's dear friend and supporter, was cynical about the value of these delegations; she wrote home to Mary Rozet Smith, "J.A. is one of the delegates to visit all the countries except Russia and Scandinavia. She wants me to go with her and of course I will. To me it seems a singularly fool performance, but I realize that the world is not all Anglo-Saxon and that other people feel very differently" (Chambers 1991, 58). During their June visits, the slaughter was at its worst, with 10,000 to 20,000 men being killed each day. Italy and Japan had been drawn into the conflict, which now raged on three continents. An entire generation of bright, hopeful young men was being destroyed: by the summer of 1916, half the graduating classes of Oxford and Cambridge were dead on the battlefields or in the field hospitals, or huddling at home as permanently maimed, disabled wrecks. Hatreds were stoked by stories of atrocities and by actual wartime hardships in the field and on the home front; vengeance and punishment as motives eclipsed any original goals, however vague in the first place. The war would drag on for another three appalling years, tearing societies apart and setting up the blasted economies of Europe for fascism and World War II.

Was continuous mediation really such an outlandish, unrealistic, unattainable alternative? Addams looked even farther ahead in her hopes after the conference, as she reported in *The Survey*: "The great achievement of this congress...is to my mind the getting together of these women from all parts of Europe, when their men-folk are shooting each other from opposite trenches. When in every warring country there is such a wonderful awakening of national consciousness flowing from heart to heart, it is a supreme effort of heroism to rise to the feeling of internationalism, without losing patriotism" (Chamberlain 1915, 220).

Tragically for Addams, her vision of the balance between patriotism and internationalism proved unacceptable even in nominally neutral America. In the single most shocking, damaging incident of her career, her honesty and compassion thrust her into a firestorm of controversy and condemnation she could never have imagined or anticipated. On July 9, 1915, newly returned from Europe, Addams addressed a crowd of over 3,000 in Carnegie Hall in New York City. Her speech was a report on the peacemaking delegations sent out by the women's congress at The Hague. As might be expected of Jane Addams, the speech was well organized, the imagery powerful, the delivery restrained and evenhanded. On all sides, she said, young men were fighting bravely and dying needlessly; the people in each belligerent country believed that they were fighting in self-defense. Addams insisted that in every country, despite severe censorship, there was what she called a "civil party"—people who recognized and deplored the power of the military and the impact of press censorship. She reserved special criticism for the pernicious, parasitic mentality that equated obedience and acceptance of violence with patriotism and an intolerance of any difference or dissent. "We were told in England that this war in essence is a conflict between militarism and democracy, but the situation is obviously not so simple as that. War itself destroys democracy wherever it thrives and tends to entrench militarism" (Addams et al. 1915, 77).

That was radical enough, a profound critique of the military erosion of civil values. But what Jane Addams reported next was even more devastating. "We heard in all countries similar statements in regard to the necessity for the use of stimulants before men would engage in bayonet charges—that they have a regular formula in Germany, that they give them rum in England and absinthe in France; that they all have to give them 'dope' before the bayonet charge is possible" (Addams 1915, 359). Addams had plenty of evidence for her observation. She cited three occasions while she was traveling with Alice Hamilton, in which a French government official, an English professor, and a wounded German soldier convalescing in a Swiss hospital had all independently described the use of stimulants. (It is most probable that the term used and adopted by Addams referred to a variety of alcoholic drinks fortified with drugs like cocaine.) The German soldier declared to Addams, "A bayonet charge does not show courage, but madness. Men must be brought to the point by stimulants, and once the charge is begun they are like insane men" ("Liquor" 1915. n.p.). In addition, Addams cited an April, 1915 letter from a French soldier, a concert oboist before the war, describing a German attack on his trench position: "This last fifteen days has been terrible here.... The Boches [Germans] have tried to mine my trench and have attacked us furiously.... They sent men to attack us right after this drunk with ether. The prisoners still had a bottle on them, partially consumed'" ("Liquor" 1915, n.p.).

Addams had mentioned the use of stimulants to demonstrate the natural revulsion for war and violence among sensitive young men; she had never intended to impugn the courage of any man. "It was taken for granted that the stimulants inhibited the sensibilities of a certain type of modern man to whom primitive warfare was especially abhorrent, although he was a brave soldier and serving his country with all his heart.... It was a thing discussed at various places where we went in Europe, quite at a matter of course. No one disputed it, or seemed to think it anything extraordinary" ("Liquor" 1915, n.p.). Indeed, the use of alcohol to desensitize and embolden soldiers is centuries old. There are descriptions of the practice in contemporary accounts of the battles of Agincourt (1415), Waterloo (1815), and the Somme (1916). There can be little doubt that Addams was right.

Nonetheless, the outcry against Addams was immediate, sustained, and nationwide. Richard Harding Davis, a militarist novelist, wrote in outrage to The New York Times that Addams had dishonored "our" soldiers and would tell orphans that their fathers had died because they were drunk. No such statement was in Addams's speech, but the feeding frenzy of the press had started and no amount of reasoned evidence or explanation could stop it. Alice Hamilton confirmed that medical journals acknowledged the open rationing of alcohol by both the German and English armies. Addams protested, "Dr. Hamilton and I had notes for each of these statements with the dates and names of the men who had made them, and it did not occur to me that the information was new or startling" (Lynd 1966, 181).

Before the war Jane Addams had been a revered, nationally beloved figure, the object of almost universal praise and approval. Her steadfast pacifism, her unflinching exposure of the ugly aspects of militarism and the experience of war, turned her almost overnight into the focus of vicious media attack and vituperative hate mail. Her very reasonableness, her refusal to demonize the Enemy, was used against her. Later, she would ruefully define freedom of the press as "the freedom to misinterpret any statement they do not like, and to suppress any statement they do not understand" (Linn [1935] 2000, 324).

Addams had become a victim of the exact processes of intolerance and mindless obedience she had so eloquently described. Her despair over the controversy left her so exhausted that she contracted pneumonia and plunged into three years of semi-invalidism. Donations to Hull-House plummeted. Illness, disapproval, and misunderstanding drove her close to self-pity and doubt; she described the plight of the pacifist in wartime: "Strangely enough he finds it possible to travel from the mire of self-pity straight to the barren hills of self-righteousness and to hate himself equally in both places" (Elshtain 2002, 232). After her death, Francis J. McConnell, Methodist Episcopal Bishop of New York City, commented that he saw this crisis as one of her finest moments. "We can well remember the howls of denial with which the militaristic patriots received this statement.... Yet anyone who got anywhere near the actual front knows that Miss Addams was speaking substantial truth.... To speak out while the battle was on was to the militarists and patrioteurs the most blasphemous of blasphemies. Miss Addams spoke out" ("Freedom" 1935, 204).

In May and June 1915, the Hague Congress sent envoys to 14 countries both belligerent and neutral: Germany, Sweden, Switzerland, Hungary, the Netherlands, Denmark, Belgium, England, France, Russia, Italy, Norway, Austria, and the United States. Addams, Aletta Jacobs, and Rosa Genori of Italy met with officials in England, Germany, Hungary, Italy, France, Belgium, the Netherlands, Switzerland, and the United States. Emily Greene Balch, Chrsytal Macmillan of Britain, Rosika Schwimmer, and Cora Romondi-Hirsch of the Netherlands visited Denmark, Norway, Sweden, and Russia. They were received by prime ministers, foreign ministers, the King of Norway, the Pope, and the presidents of Switzerland and the United States. In a total of 35 meetings with these government officials, they urged the creation of a sitting council of neutral nations to provide the practical machinery to resolve disputes nonviolently. Privately, even belligerent representatives treated them with courtesy and seemed willing at least to regard their proposals seriously; one unnamed prime minister commented, "Yours is the sanest proposal that has been brought to this office in the last six months" (Foster 1989, 206). But in public, combatants believed that they could not afford to negotiate from a position of any perceived weakness. That awful summer, the Germans seemed to have a slight upper hand and were more hospitable to possible peace proposals. As historian Walter Millis bitterly commented later, "it was in the pacific democracies of the Entente that the very mention of the word 'peace' was becoming a crime against the state" (Millis 1935, 225).

The great hope of the mediation movement was American president Woodrow Wilson, a stern, high-minded, intellectual moralist. Addams met with Wilson on six separate occasions between July and December 1915, often with the strong support of his advisers. One such adviser, Charles R. Crane, commented to Wilson, "Of course she is the best we have and has been received everywhere as a spiritual messenger... Added to her great spiritual power is wonderful wisdom and discretion. Every woman in the land and most men would be cheered by knowing that you and she were in conference" (De Benedetti 1986, 38).

Tragically, Wilson had already decided against mediation. The British passenger ship *Lusitania* had been sunk by German submarines off the coast of Ireland on May 7, 1915, with a loss of 128 U.S. citizens, and public opinion cried for revenge. (It has since been proven that the *Lusitania* was also carrying an illicit cargo of arms from U.S. manufacturers to England.) Wilson resisted the idea of mediation for complicated reasons. He was a rigid, fervid moralist who longed to save the situation through the power of his own speech and ideals. He had no prior political experience and no familiarity with collaboration or compromise, exactly the skills most vital to nonviolent conflict resolution. After a visit from Addams in August 1915, Wilson wrote to his fiancée, "I can't see it. And I am quite sure that they [Addams and her associates] consider me either very dull, very deep, or very callous" (Millis 1935, 2).

Addams's expectations and persistence frustrated and may even have angered Wilson, who was moving steadily toward a position of preparedness that made American entry into the war virtually inevitable. James Linn believed that Wilson's attitude doomed the mediation movement: "The determining factor... in President Wilson's disinclination to discuss the matter of 'continuous mediation' was President Wilson. The plan involved the cooperation of many neutral nations, and the President was not by nature willing to cooperate. He must not only lead; he must act alone.... He had no eagerness for work with others, and no skill in such work" (Linn [1935] 2000, 315).

This monumental early drive for a mediated solution to the conflict was a failure. In October 1915, the executive committee of the women's congress issued a despairing statement: "The excruciating burden of responsibility for the hopeless continuance of this war no longer rests on the will of the belligerent nations alone. It rests also on the will of those neutral governments and peoples who have been spared its shock but cannot, if they would, absolve themselves from their full responsibility for the continuance of war" (Foster 1989, 208).

Addams had another meeting with Wilson in November, still trying to hope that she might move him somehow. She never stood a chance. By this point Wilson was relying heavily on his close friend and adviser, Edward M. House, a wealthy Texan with close ties to munitions manufacturers and other war profiteers. House was determined to get the United States into the war on the British side, and he openly belittled the peace advocates. He was especially disdainful of Addams, Lillian Wald, and Rosika Schwimmer; he recorded in his journal afterwards, "As usual, I got them into a controversy among themselves, which delights me" (Millis 1935, 234). After House's rebuff, Addams went public and organized a massive telegraph campaign among thousands of women's clubs, deluging Wilson with telegrams demanding a neutral mediation conference; the White House had to hire extra telegraph clerks to handle the volume.

Addams and her pacifist allies were up against overwhelming forces. Later that month President Wilson made a major speech in New York, publicly committing the United States to preparedness: "We have it in mind to be prepared, but not for war, but only for defence [sic]..." (Millis 1935, 237). The language was still carefully couched in self-defense, but the full-scale militarization of American society was well under way. All the major corporations in industry and banking were by then deeply invested in the war and counting on additional business. "Preparedness" was a code word for massive increases in the military budget.

Addams was at her best testifying before committees. She was precise, analytic, well informed, respectful, but unshakeable in her convictions. Her delivery was low-key, letting the facts generate the outrage they deserved. Her dignified, controlled oratory led one long-time friend to refer to her as a "statesman and not a politician" (Gilman 1948, 5). Addams testified before the House Foreign Affairs Committee in January 1916, urging Federal protection of the foreign-born prior to naturalization. She argued for a Federal minimum wage and forcefully delineated the dark connections between the enormous profits from foreign investments and the demands that the Army and Navy protect those investments. (The full, shabby picture of national military force employed in the service of private industry emerges with startling contemporary relevance in the later, bitter comments of Smedley Butler, who had led the American Marines' occupation of Haiti in 1915:

I helped make Mexico safe for American oil interests in 1914. I helped make Haiti and Cuba a decent place for the National City Bank boys to collect revenues in.... I helped purify Nicaragua for the international banking house of Brown Brothers.... I brought light to the Dominican Republic for American sugar interests in 1916. I helped make Honduras "right" for American fruit companies in 1903. In China in 1927 I helped see to it that Standard Oil went its way unmolested. Looking back on it, I feel I might have given Al Capone a few hints.") (Berson 1994, 28)

Addams also testified before the House Committee on Military Affairs that month, warning of the dangers of an arms race and urging the Congress to resist calls for increased military expenditures. In her customary logical, thorough manner, she suggested the formation of an independent commission to investigate the efficiency of current Army and Navy spending, which stood even then at 30 percent of Federal income.

With gentle reproach, Addams suggested that war hysteria seemed to hit men primarily: "I do not like to say that men are more emotional than women, but whenever I go to a national political convention and hear men cheering for a candidate for 1 hour and 15 minutes it seems to me that perhaps men are somewhat emotional.... They are much more likely to catch this war spirit and respond to this panic" ("Statement" 1916, 5). When her deliberate reversal of the gender stereotypes affronted the committee members (as she must have known it would), she added, "I want to assure you, of course, that I am not addressing myself to the gentlemen of this committee who, I am sure, are exceptions to any such unbalanced tendency" ("Statement" 1916, 7).

There had been a concentrated effort to draw the United States into the war since its beginning. In 1915 a book appeared entitled *Defenseless America,* depicting a passive America overrun by gross German brutes. Its author, Hudson Maxim, was coincidentally a manufacturer of high explosives who admitted that he wanted to "help Congressional appropriations for defense." (Maxim's brother in England manufactured the new machine guns British soldiers were carrying into battle.) The popular book was quickly turned into a gory motion picture oddly called "The Battle Cry of Peace," which starred Norma Talmadge suffering "the agonies of an invasion far more horrible—and more exciting—than anything depicted in the censored films of the real war in Europe" (Millis 1935, 217).

The public response was swift and predictable. Even before Wilson asked Congress for a declaration of war early in April 1917, the propaganda industry was in full operation. The ostensibly independent Committee on Public Information churned out fiercely paranoid pamphlets, maintained a large bureau of trained amateur inspirational speakers, and produced pro-war films with inflammatory titles like "The Prussian Cur" and "The Beast of Berlin." The new definition of patriotism in wartime demanded a total suspension of individual conscience, unthinking loyalty to the official position, and an Orwellian attention to "correct" language and expression.

Wilson campaigned for reelection in 1916 under the slogan "He kept us out of war." Addams, who had backed Theodore Roosevelt and the Progressive Party in 1912, now endorsed Wilson, and he sent her a warm note of thanks after his victory. In January he gave a ringing speech to Congress arguing that no militarily imposed victory could last: "Victory would mean a peace forced upon a loser, a victor's terms forced upon the vanquished. It would be accepted in humiliation under duress, at an intolerable sacrifice, and would leave a sting, a resentment, a bitter memory upon which the terms of peace would rest, not permanently, but only as upon quicksand" (De Benedetti 1986, 45).

That same month Germany announced the resumption of unrestricted submarine warfare. In February an American ship was sunk off England, and Wilson broke off diplomatic relations with Germany. When Addams and other peace advocates visited Wilson in February, she warned him that his social reforms would be overshadowed by the horrors of war. He argued that adjudication was no longer possible, and that the United States had to go to war so that he could be part of the peace negotiations, a role that would be denied him if the country maintained neutrality. Several years later Addams reflected that he valued his own leadership too highly: "Was it a result of my bitter disappointment that I hotly and no doubt unfairly asked myself whether any had the right to rate his moral leadership so high that he could consider the sacrifice of the lives of thousands of his young countrymen a necessity?" (Chambers 1991, 108). On February 14, 1917, Congress passed the Threats Against the President Act, making it treason to criticize Wilson in any way.

On March 15, 1917, the Czar of Russia abdicated, leaving the Eastern front in chaos and the German position greatly strengthened. That same week three more American ships were sunk. Wilson was under mounting pressure to go to war. He finally succumbed, with seeming reluctance, horrified at the prospect. In the early morning of April 2, 1917, he struggled with the request he was scheduled to make to Congress only a few hours later. Sounding eerily like Jane Addams on militarism, he commented mournfully to an old friend who was staying with him through that bitter night, "Once lead this people into war and they'll forget there ever was such a thing as tolerance. To fight you must be brutal and ruthless, and the spirit of ruthless brutality will enter into the very fibre of our national life, infecting Congress, the courts, the policeman on the beat, the man in the street" (Millis 1935, 430).

The next morning Wilson asked a special session of Congress to declare war. The chamber erupted into wild, inappropriate cheering, although a few sober members recognized the gravity of the moment. Senator Robert La Follette of Wisconsin spoke for the opposition: "Mr. President, I had supposed until recently that it was the duty of Senators and Representatives in Congress to vote and act according to their convictions.... Quite another doctrine has recently been promulgated...and that is the doctrine of 'stand back of the President' without inquiring whether the President is right or wrong." George W. Norris of Nebraska, another antiwar voice, was even more blunt. He declared that the war had been forced upon the country to increase the profits of stockbrokers and munitions manufacturers and dealers: "We are going into war at the command of gold.... I feel that we are about to put the dollar sign upon the American flag" (Millis 1935, 449, 450). Another senator accused Norris of treason and a shouting match ensued.

In the House of Representatives, one Representative declared that most members and their constituents were against the war but were afraid to say so in public; he said that a secret vote would defeat the war resolution. The House debated for almost 17 hours without a break. Jeannette Rankin, the only woman in Congress, was a reform Republican from Montana, where populist sentiment was against entry into the war; in addition, she was herself a committed pacifist. Nonetheless, she was under enormous pressure to vote for the declaration of war—ironically, the worst pressure was from women's groups who were desperate to shed the label of weakness and sentimentality. At the last minute on the second roll call on the war resolution, Rankin courageously cast her vote against entry into the war. Contrary to newspaper reports, she did not weep: "I had wept so much that week that my tears were all gone by the time the vote came" (Berson 1994, 249). Alone among 50 antiwar votes, Rankin was subjected to personal vilification and slander. The final roll call saw 6 Senators and 50 Representatives opposed to the resolution. On April 6, 1917, the United States declared war on Germany and its allies.

All the hostilities and intolerance that Addams had warned about exploded in ugly forms throughout the country. In June the Espionage Bill set a fine of up to $10,000 and 20 years in prison for disloyalty, refusal to serve in the armed forces, interfering with recruitment or enlistment of soldiers, or aiding the enemy "in any way." Any dissenting publications were banned from the mails. All minority groups—immigrants, women, African Americans, labor, socialists—struggled to define and demonstrate their own loyalties. A rumor swept across the South in 1917 that the Germans were planning to back an insurrection of African Americans that would claim Texas as a black republic where Mexicans and Asians would be treated as equals (considered a nightmare).

Under the very real fear of lynching, black leaders scrambled to prove themselves loyal and uncomplaining. Black Americans flocked north to work in the expanding wartime factories. The factory owners used African Americans as strikebreakers against the struggling labor unions, generating enormous resentment, rage, and violence—even though the unions refused outright to accept blacks as members. In 1917, 38 African Americans lost their lives to lynching parties. The following year the figure almost doubled; in 1919 more than 70 African Americans died in lynchings, while many more were killed in incoherent mob violence.

Anti-immigrant sentiment was especially virulent. Congress passed a bill in 1917 requiring a literacy test as part of any immigration application, although this same Congress rejected any appropriations to the Bureau of Education to help immigrants learn English. Immigrants were all suspect, but those from Central Europe, even after several generations, were especially hated and feared. In April 1918 Robert Praeger, a young German-born immigrant, attempted to enlist in the U.S. Army in St. Louis, Missouri. For this affront, he was stripped naked by a mob, tied up with an American flag, dragged through the streets, beaten, and finally lynched. At their trial, his murderers wore red, white, and blue ribbons on their lapels and described themselves as heroic defenders of the homeland; their lawyers referred to the lynching as "patriotic murder." The jury took 25 minutes to find them not guilty.

Throughout this sustained nightmare of irrational hatred, Jane Addams did not waver. She never lost sight of her real goals, and she never stopped offering society the vision of cooperative, compassionate, mutually sustaining human beings. Less than 2 weeks after the war resolution had passed, Addams addressed the Chicago Woman's Club: "That the United States has entered the war has not changed my views on the invalidity of war as a method of settlement of social problems a particle, and

I can see no reason why one should not so what one believes in time of war as in time of peace...." (Linn [1935] 2000, 330).

In the most ringing terms, Addams continued to speak her mind. In "Patriotism and Pacifists in Wartime," written in the summer of 1917, she argued that the formation of truly international structures of government would be able to render war obsolete: "What we insist upon is that the world can be organized politically by its statesmen as it has been already organized into an international fiscal structure by its bankers or into an international scientific association by its scientists.... The very breakdown exhibited by the present war reinforces the pacifists' contention that there is need of an international charter...of international rights, to be issued by the nations great and small, with large provisions for economic freedom" (Chambers 1991, 120).

Addams herself sought to be both consistent with her pacifist principles and useful to her country in this crisis. In August 1917 Congress established the Department of Food Administration (DFA), headed by Herbert Hoover, to address the growing food shortages throughout Europe. Addams was deeply committed to the concept of food relief, and she could feel that her work on this was consonant with her pacifism. Throughout the war she worked with the DFA and with the American friends Service Committee, touring the country, speaking to raise awareness of the need for food conservation. The mission was well-suited to Addams, who had always envisioned a literal connection between Peace and Bread. The response to these pressing humanitarian needs started in daily activities, in the kind of shared human tasks that transcended nationalism and would, she believed, lead to renewed moral energy and deeper understanding. She saw as well the central role that food would play in rebuilding the life of Europe after the War; she hoped that the international organization growing up around the delivery of food would serve as a template for future international structures. In her tours and public speeches, Addams constantly returned to the image of Woman as the planter and reaper of wheat, the baker and distributor of the basic stuff of life. To her, feminism—the honoring of the female element of life—was inextricably bound to an antimilitarist stance. In *The Long Road of Woman's Memory*, written during the war, she declared, "It would be absurd for women even to suggest equal rights in a world run solely by physical force, and Feminism must necessarily assert the ultimate supremacy of moral agencies" (Addams 1916, 129).

The rest of Addams's life would be consumed in the complex challenge of maintaining her integrity while struggling to ensure the survival of

Hull-House and also to be of meaningful service to the America she still believed in. She walked a delicate tightrope at Hull-House those years. Most of the male residents supported the war; 8 of the residents under the age of 30 enlisted in the armed forces, and 6 were sent overseas. Most of the female residents were not pacifists, either, and the neighborhood in general caught the mood of jingoistic, prowar hysteria. Despite her own sentiments, Addams was careful not to attempt to impose her philosophy on any one else, to honor the individual decisions that residents and neighbors made. Hull-House provided lavish farewell dinners for neighborhood boys before they shipped out; the house itself was an accepted site for final goodbyes.

Addams remained a remarkably tolerant pacifist. Dorothy Detzer was a teenager living at Hull-House when the United States declared war; her twin brother hurried to enlist. She recalled how proud she was of him, and that Addams had assured her that she was entitled to her pride. Addams never brought up the issue of her own pacifism. A few years after the war, Detzer's brother died from lung damage inflicted by poison gas. Detzer did famine relief work in Europe in 1920 and became a confirmed pacifist herself; in 1924 she became executive secretary of the Women's International League for Peace and Freedom. It was years later before she realized how rare and open Addams's attitude had been, how utterly free of superiority or righteousness. "I did not then appreciate what it meant—this residence, with pacifists and non-pacifists living together in a spirit of tolerance and good will. It was only a quality such as hers which could have made this possible" (Detzer 1938, 5).

Chapter 8

ZURICH, 1919, AND BEYOND: FAITH STRUGGLES

Finally, at the 11th hour of the 11th day of the 11th month of 1918, as randomly and as meaninglessly as it had begun, the First World War ended. The humanitarian situation throughout Europe, but especially in the defeated countries, was desperate. The day after the Armistice, November 12, 1918, leading German women's activists sent a telegram to Edith Wilson, wife of President Wilson, appealing for emergency aid. A similar telegram, sent to Jane Addams, was intercepted by the State Department and released to American newspapers by the War Department; Addams herself read of this telegram in the press. The German women urged "their American sisters to intercede for relief of truce conditions regarding terms of demobilization, blockade, wagons, locomotives. We are all free voters of a free republic now, greeting you heartily" (Sklar et al. 1998, 228). Addams responded with gentle public support, all she could do, since the Trading with the Enemy Act forbade any private communication with anyone in Germany. While a few liberal papers expressed sympathy, most of the press was hostile and openly contemptuous of the very concept of German suffering. The *Boston Evening Record* scoffed, "The world is quite justified now in suspecting that behind this row of wailing German women the Hun hides treachery and lies" (Davis 1973, 252).

Immediately, the International Committee of Women for Permanent Peace called a conference to be held in Zurich, Switzerland, in May 1919, at the same time that the military victors were designing their peace treaty at Versailles. The gathering had first been scheduled to meet in France, but was relocated when the French government refused to permit delegates from defeated nations to attend.

The American delegation was led by Jane Addams, who had been elected president of the committee; as president of what would soon become the Women's International League for Peace and Freedom (WILPF), she would chair six more such conference throughout the 1920s, until ill health forced her to step down in 1929. Delegates included Florence Kelley, Alice Hamilton, Lillian Wald, and the infamous pacifist congresswoman Jeannette Rankin. The Americans went first to France: to Paris, and then on a heart-breaking tour of several utterly blasted, devastated battlefields. At Argonne, Addams managed to find the grave of her nephew John Linn, who had been killed in battle there. Grieving and sober, the women journeyed on to Zurich, where further signs of destruction, famine, and disease abounded.

It was a somber group of 136 women from 14 countries who convened in Zurich on May 12, 1919. They had no illusions about the magnitude of the crisis before them, but that scale only increased their sense of urgent responsibility. As president of the Congress, Addams bluntly acknowledged the terrible frustrations of the last conference's mediation efforts, while insistently holding out equal parts of hope and hard work: "After all, what did these things effect? Our efforts with the neutral countries were entirely vain.... At least we did this, we made a similar public opinion in the 14 countries from which the women came to The Hague, and we have to go back and make a similar public opinion upon the resolutions which we may put forward from this congress" (*Report* 1920, 196). She declared, with some justification, that the program the mediation proponents had advocated in 1915 had influenced President Wilson's Fourteen Points, which he was urging the Versailles negotiators to adopt.

The delegates at the Zurich conference were highly educated, experienced, outspoken, audacious women. As Mary Chamberlain reported in *The Survey,* "The women at the conference were the outsiders, the visionaries you might call them, who had clung to their ideals throughout the war. Several of the Germans had been imprisoned for opposing the war, many had been persecuted; practically all, from all countries, had been discredited for their principles" (Sklar et al. 1998, 235). Their opening statement declared the breadth of their outrage with the current situation: "The events of the last four years have proved that our civilization has completely failed. Our lives have been dominated by a purely materialistic philosophy, by a policy of sheer force and violence" (*Report* 1920, 131).

Indeed, the Zurich congress seemed to take a more profoundly radical perspective on the real needs of the world than these same women had at

The Hague. Addams appealed for peace in the context of the experience of its absence; her arguments were neither dogmatic nor religious, but always grounded in human need and ethical response. The various sessions of the congress addressed an astonishing range of social, economic, and educational programs. Their proposals were always detailed, specific, based on careful analysis. They recommended international labor regulations, minimum wage, safety standards, adjustments for seasonal labor and overtime, standards to protect pregnant workers, guaranteed pre- and postnatal care, and paid maternity leave. They urged that no child under the age of 15 be employed anywhere, and that education be free and compulsory until the age of 15, and free thereafter until the age of 18.

Much of the work of the Congress focused on drafts they had obtained of the Treaty of Versailles and of the tentative covenant of the League of Nations. The Congress examined these drafts with enormous effort and diligence. As Addams reported in her opening remarks:

> Because many of the documents came so late, because it has been impossible to prepare for the Congress as in ordinary times when the methods of communication are all open, it has not been feasible to present a detailed agenda. The printed slip you already have is therefore a mere outline, all too meager. But copies of the resolutions in French, German, and English as finally reported by the sub-committees and passed upon by the Executive Committee as a whole will be placed in the hands of every delegate at the opening of each morning session, that she may have before her the material for the day. (*Report* 1920, 2)

The Woman's Peace Party had urged some sort of international organization since 1915, but its support for the League of Nations was guarded and critical; the proposed covenant ignored political equity, economic justice, and the need to abrogate existing treaties that facilitated unfair regional powers. Addams and her colleagues insisted on the need for real disarmament (including a program to restrict the manufacture of arms), an end to all conscription, a world court, amnesty for all conscientious objectors, and significant protections for women and children. They urged the elimination of capitalist control over other countries' resources.

Addams was, as always, concerned with the potential for increasing human understanding and tolerance. Reflecting her priorities, the congress examined the role of misunderstanding in the recent war; it condemned unequivocally any government propaganda, censorship, interference with private correspondence, any restraints on the free expression of public opinion. "The women of this International Congress," Addams declared, "have become convinced, especially by their experience of the last five years, that this misleading of the popular understanding is one of the greatest dangers to human welfare" (*Report* 1920, 260).

A major unifying concern of the 1919 Congress was the status of women worldwide. These educated, privileged women were deeply committed to the welfare of all their sisters. They argued presciently that the social, legal, and economic rights of women were sure indicators of the general level well-being in any society, although they did "recognize that differences in social development and tradition make strict uniformity with respect to the status of women difficult of immediate attainment" (*Report* 1920, 247).

The Zurich Congress turned its attention as well to the desperate food shortages throughout Central Europe. The Allies had imposed a blockade on Germany during the war, and insisted on maintaining the blockade after the Armistice as a means of forcing Germany to accept the Treaty of Versailles. Famine and disease were rampant across Central Europe, and the Congress called for immediate action in the name of humanity. On May 13, 1919, Addams telegraphed Wilson at Versailles, urging that the blockade be lifted at once, and that international priority be assigned to providing the necessary resources and transportation, that "luxuries shall not be given transport from one country to another until the necessaries of life are supplied to all and that the people of every country be rationed in order that all the starving shall be fed." Gracious as always but noncommittal, Wilson responded, "Your message appeals both to my head and to my heart and I hope most sincerely that means may be found, though the present outlook is extremely unpromising because of infinite practical difficulties" (Chambers 1991, 159). The mood at Versailles was one of rabid vengeance; the starving dying children of Central Europe were no more than instruments toward that punishment.

The Congress was even more critical of the Treaty: "This International Congress of Women expresses its deep regret that the terms of peace proposed at Versailles should so seriously violate the principles upon which alone a just and lasting peace can be secured, and which the democracies of the world had come to accept" (*Report* 1920, 60). The Treaty tacitly honored secret treaties that recognized the colonial interests of Japan and France in violation of the victors' publicly stated principles of self-determination. The lopsided disarmament requirements and the draconian economic and financial sanctions against the vanquished seemed to ensure that poverty, disease, and festering resentment were bound to spread. One of the Congress's most radical resolutions called for an independent commission to investigate war profiteering internationally. Addams, as President of the Congress, and five other delegates traveled to Versailles to present a full draft of their critique of the treaty.

The United States never ratified the Treaty of Versailles. For most of 1919 the treaty was blocked in the Senate Foreign Relations Committee, chaired by the isolationist, conservative Henry Cabot Lodge. Industrialists Andrew Mellon and Henry Frick financed a massive public campaign against it. In October 1919 Wilson suffered a paralyzing stroke from which he never fully recovered, although the extent of his incapacity was kept from the public and he never delegated authority to his vice president. He was left with no energy, no ability to concentrate on complexities, unable to negotiate for ratification with the Senate. In repeated votes, the Senate couldn't even find a simple majority in favor of the treaty, let alone the two-thirds majority required for ratification. Finally, in 1921, President Warren G. Harding signed a separate peace treaty with Germany. Similarly, the United States never joined the League of Nations nor recognized the World Court established at The Hague.

Addams's closing words to the Congress were as realistic and yet hopeful as her opening remarks had been. She acknowledged her profound disappointment with the Treaty of Versailles, but spoke also of continuing to work in the hope for understanding and of the "moral energy" of common humanity:

> So I bid you go forth to this great task, and we shall all know that we have this sisterhood and comradeship together, and we shall come back to the next Congress and tell of our failures, and also may be tell of success. Whether we fail or not, we know that we have the clue, and the military way will have to come to an end, if only because it has tried to do what could not be done except by spiritual power, and so has ruined itself. (*Report* 1920, 238)

After the Congress had closed, most of the American delegates sailed home. Florence Kelley, on her way home, wrote vividly to Mary Rozet Smith of Jane Addams in action in Zurich. She admitted that at first she had been skeptical and reluctant to attend, "But next time I would go on my knees. It was *unbelievably wonderful*. . . . Needless to say, J. A. presided to

the satisfaction of everyone.... I heard people say in the English delegation 'What an excellent chairman, so fair, and not a moment wasted.'"
Kelley reported many other comments on Addams's great organization,
flexibility, and modesty. "'I'm sorry I made that blunder'—I shall always
hear her saying that, *and* she makes so few blunders.... J.A. was at her
very best. She loved the whole undertaking" (JAMSS).

Addams and Alice Hamilton did not return to the United States with
the other delegates. Ever concerned with famine, they joined an American Friends mission poised to deliver $30,000 worth of food to Germany.
Herbert Hoover, then head of the American Relief Association in Europe, insisted that the hunger volunteers wait in Paris until Germany ratified the Treaty of Versailles. On July 7, 1919, barely five days after that
ratification, Addams and Hamilton traveled into Germany on the first
civilian passports issued to Americans.

There is a complex web of connection and consequence in maintaining food delivery to any urban, industrialized country, but especially one
that had been shattered by the war. Addams and Hamilton reported that
the Germans and Austrians were unable to import decent fodder for their
cattle, as they had done before the war. The cows were also suffering from
deprivation, fed inadequately on potato parings and giving less than one-
third of their normal yield of milk; in some areas milk production was
down by almost 90 percent. At the Zurich conference a German delegate,
Dr. Helen Stockner, had reported that 50 percent of the babies born in
Berlin in 1918–1919 had died. Conditions in Austria were even worse.
Malnourishment, typhus, tuberculosis, rickets, and skin diseases were
among the afflictions rampant, especially among the very young and old.
Any sort of fuel, heating or cooking, was in desperately short supply.
"Dresden is *cold* and *dark*," reported one Quaker volunteer. "Never before
have I been in such a dark place at night. The thing that is working here
is unrelenting hunger." Addams reported from Vienna, "The tragedy of
Vienna is so vast and so multiform that it appalls the imagination—cold,
darkness, disease, carnal misery, spiritual anguish, hunger of the body and
hunger of the heart, all combine to make the city an inferno." Another
volunteer declared, "If people in America had any idea of the awful situation over here you could not stop them from pouring into the feeding
fund every cent they could spare" (JAMSS). By the summer of 1920, the
Quakers were running 3,400 soup kitchens in Central Europe, serving
600,000 meals a day to children and adolescents.

Jane Addams was determined that people in America should learn
about the desperate situation in the defeated countries; she and Hamilton

returned home to spread the word. As she reported in *The Survey*, "Our impressions crowded each other so fast that they merged into one, an impression of mass hunger as we had never imagined it, hunger of millions continued month after month for three years or more…" (Sklar et al. 1998, 231). She was deeply shocked by the response she got. The American press condemned the Treaty of Versailles as too lenient. Addams, on a speaking tour to raise awareness of the starving children she had seen, was often shouted down as a traitor; in Detroit, she was heckled for 45 minutes. She was excoriated in the Chicago newspapers, and she began receiving vicious hate mail.

It was considered especially damning that Addams advocated emergency food and medical relief for the new Soviet Union, which was staggering from the effects of brutal civil war in addition to the Great War. The fear of anything radical had been manipulated to such a level in America that no such outreach could be considered rationally. Addams kept trying to keep attention focused on human need. "You can be as savagely anti-Bolshevik as you please," she wrote in the Cincinnati *Post* in 1921, "but you can't or shouldn't be anti-human" (Farrell 1967, 187). Associates of Addams's supported her and defended the aid she had arranged for Russia; Emily Greene Balch wrote, "The relief with which Miss Addams was connected was absolutely unpolitical and administered purely from motives of compassion with extraordinary conscientiousness and effectiveness. Who wants to punish starving children for their parents' politics?" (Balch 1927, 3). Tragically, the vast majority of Americans seemed to want exactly that. Addams's outspoken efforts for apolitical famine relief were held against her and would become part of the dangerous radicalism of which she was accused.

Addams's ethical and social positions were remarkably consistent throughout her public life; what shifted around her was public opinion driven largely, in those years before radio and television, by a highly reactionary popular press. In her polite, calm way, Addams had always been willing to take on unpopular causes. Her commitment to immigrants' rights brought her into frequent conflict with the xenophobic tendencies of American society.

In 1901 President William McKinley was assassinated by Leon Czolgolz, a professed anarchist, and a wave of panicked arrests of anarchists swept the country. The first arrested in Chicago was Abraham Isaak, a Russian Jew and editor of an anarchist newspaper, who had often visited Hull-House; Addams knew him and thought of him as a gifted scholar. When word of his arrest reached Hull-House early on a Sunday morning,

Addams hurried to the home of the mayor of Chicago to demand his release. At first the mayor refused even to permit Isaak access to a lawyer, but he did allow Addams to see him in prison. Arguing with her famous genteel stubbornness, Addams was able to get a lawyer for Isaak, and he was soon released without charges. Piqued, the mayor alerted the press to Addams's role. When Addams returned to Hull-House after securing Isaak's release, she found a swarm of predatory reporters waiting for her. Despite Isaak's innocence, Addams's support for him drew further right wing wrath upon her; wealthy patrons withdrew pledges and Hull-House suffered substantial financial losses. Addams received additional hate mail, now including death threats. She never wavered in her support for due process.

Understandably, Addams's commitment to supporting immigrants dated virtually from the founding of Hull-House. The goal of Americanization could be defined both positively and negatively: right wing, nativist groups feared discontent and the radical political movements of Europe, and they demanded obedience and rigid submission to the status quo as American; on the other hand, Addams welcomed a large degree of diversity and what she called "immigrant gifts," traditions and skills from the Old World, and she believed that a wide embrace of true American values included freedom of expression. Addams observed sadly that immigrants seemed to absorb the negative racial attitudes of American society: In the summer of 1921 an African American man was lynched in an Italian neighborhood close to Hull-House, and a friend of Addams's commented, "Of course this would never have happened in Italy; they are becoming Americanized" (Elshtain 2002, 209).

Public fear and hysteria were generated by the War and the Russian Revolution and further manipulated by unscrupulous politicians. Paranoid groups proliferated, with names like the Liberty League, American Defense Society, National Security League, Sentinels of the Republic, National Association for Constitutional Government, United States Flag Association, Women Builders of America, Better America Federation, and such older organizations as the Daughters of the American Revolution and the American Legion. From 1918 throughout the 1920s, the Department of Justice supported nongovernmental super-patriot groups and vigilantes like the American Protective League, who spied on their neighbors, opened other people's mail, led extralegal raids, and incited rabid anti-German sentiment. Chicago, with its high proportion of Central European immigrants and its Populist labor history, suffered especially virulent hysteria. The poet Edgar Lee Masters recalled later "an orgy of hate and hypocrisy, cruelty and revenge.... Scarcely a human being in the city was left untouched by mania, unless it was the magnates who profited by this slaughter in Europe; and, as to them, they suffered an accession of greed which might be called insanity" (Farrell 1967, 173). In the Hull-House neighborhood Chicago police broke into homes without warrants, beat residents, and packed them randomly into patrol wagons and then to jail.

Mass deportations escalated an atmosphere of poisonous fear and suspicion. In 1918, 11,625 immigrant aliens were deported from Chicago alone; reentry into the United States after deportation was a felony offense. There was no appeal, no recourse; families were torn apart, American-born children stranded when their parents were deported. By 1920 the uncertainty and injustice had driven over 1.5 million immigrants to apply for return passage to Europe, despite its war-ravaged conditions. Addams condemned these ideologically driven mass arrests as "a dangerous departure from the Anglo-Saxon tradition of arresting a man for his overt act and not for his opinions" (Addams 1920a, n.p.). Throughout the period of the infamous "Palmer Raids" (named after the reactionary Attorney General, A. Mitchell Palmer), Addams was unwavering and vocal in her support of immigrants' and even radicals' rights.

The Quota Act of 1921 established the National origins Quota System and cut off further Mediterranean and Slavic immigration. Addams declared that the war had brought on a terribly damaging dominance by a misled majority over individual rights: "America fell back into the old habit of judging men, not by their individual merits or capacities, but by the categories of race and religion" (Addams 1922a, 116).

Jane Addams, middle class America's secular saint and most honored woman, was about to be cast as the utter opposite: dangerous, unpatriotic, devious, Un-American. Her own positions on controversial issues hadn't changed, but the political landscape had shifted so far to the right that she could be perceived as too radical, too challenging. In a letter to the editor of the *Chicago Tribune* on February 24, 1920, she condemned the Justice Department's raids, mass arrests, and deportations: "The cure for the spirit of unrest in this country is conciliation and education—not hysteria. Free speech is the greatest safety valve of our United States. Let us give these people a chance to explain their beliefs and desires. Let us end this suppression and spirit of intolerance which is making America another autocracy" (JAMSS). Predictably, the response to her plea was another wave of hate mail.

Addams argued that the American experience of the Great War was very different from Europe's—the United States had entered the war late, had never been invaded, and lacked the same sense of devastation and horror. She recalled how she had attended a huge peace rally in London's Trafalgar Square in 1919, right after the war, in which fully half of the demonstrators were returning soldiers who knew the cost of war firsthand. But thousands of young American men had enlisted without ever getting shipped overseas; they were still full of an immature martial spirit untempered by reality or tragedy.

With great compassion and insight, Addams dissected the emotional and psychological sources of the rampant fear and anxiety after the war: "The war had made obvious the sheer inability of the world to prevent terror and misery. It had been a great revelation of feebleness, as if weakness, ignorance, and overwhelming nationalism had combined to produce something much more cruel than any calculated cruelty could have been" (Addams 1922a, 118).

Regarding the Justice Department's blatantly un-Constitutional attacks on any form of dissent, she declared that nationalism had become a dangerous religion in America: "the nation demands worship and devotion for its own sake, as if it existed irrespective of the tests of reality. It demands unqualified obedience, denounces all who differ as heretics, insists that it alone has the truth, and exhibits all the well-known signs of dogmatism" (Addams 1920b, 525).

Addams's anguish was well-founded. Under Federal and state statutes passed during the war, over 4,000 people were imprisoned under the vague category of "wartime offenders." They included "absolute" conscientious objectors, labor activists, and anyone accused of making statements that might be deemed to discourage recruitment or interfere with the draft.

In Chicago in 1919, 100 members of the radical labor union International Workers of the World (IWW, or "Wobblies") were arrested and charged with sedition; their bail was set ridiculously high and they had difficulty finding legal representation. They spent months in the Cook County jail under hideous conditions: 1 man died in jail, 1 went insane, and 11 contracted tuberculosis. Finally, a judge lowered their bail, but even after bail was posted, most of the released men had nowhere to stay. Addams worked to raise money for food and shelter for the Wobblies. She worried a little about their angry, fairly violent rhetoric and philosophy, but she responded as always to need on a straightforward humanitarian basis despite the controversy. "No one else touched the situation in Chicago," she recalled in *The Aftermath of War* (Addams 1922a, 117).

Addams never allowed nationalism to limit her vision of human rights. She was involved in wartime efforts to free conscientious objectors in England as well as in the United States. After the Armistice Addams was a leader in the campaign to grant amnesty to all political prisoners, but Attorney General A. Mitchell Palmer refused to consider the idea.

Government harassment of Jane Addams began in 1919. Archibald Stevenson was a New York lawyer who had been hired by the Military Intelligence Division of the War Department to investigate radicals. In January 1919 he testified before a Senate subcommittee about his work and produced a list of 62 people he considered "dangerous, destructive, and anarchistic" (Alonso 1993, 129). Jane Addams was at the top of the list, which included some of the most prominent and respected figures in American reform. (25 percent of the people so named were women.)

There was considerable protest against the so-called disloyal list. Paul Kellogg, editor of *The Survey*, called on Secretary of War Newton Baker to repudiate "that indiscriminate, brutally unjust, fool-in-the-head list of Americans put under the ban by the Military Intelligence Division of the United States War Department at the Senate hearing yesterday" ("Stevenson's" 1919, n.p.). Shortly thereafter, Baker denied publicly that Stevenson had ever been an employee of the Military Intelligence Division, and he expressed disapproval of the entire concept of such a list. He singled Addams out for particular notice: "Miss Jane Addams, for instance, lends dignity and greatness to any list in which her name appears (*The New York Times*, January 27, 1919). In reality, Baker was being disingenuous: Stevenson was technically paid by the Justice Department, and the Military Intelligence Division had borrowed him for this assignment. The press seized on the list with glee nonetheless. Addams and the women's peace efforts during the war were held up to merciless ridicule.

In the hysteria, New York State authorized State Senator Clayton R. Lusk to carry out a full investigation of "revolutionary radicalism." In 1920 the Lusk Commission produced a four-volume report, a bizarre mixture of random documents wildly misinterpreted and wild, outright falsehoods, which defamed a wide range of intellectuals, reformers, peace workers, and others. Lusk accused Addams of using the women's peace movement to further her socialist goals; he also condemned Addams for her efforts against child labor.

All the old, unresolved hatred of Addams, festering since her "stimulants" statement in 1915, came roaring back. The paranoid lists and charts delineating alleged conspiracies proliferated. One of them depicted a gigantic spiderweb of interconnected radical associations, which attacked every liberal, human rights, labor rights, and children's rights organization in the country and condemned over 100 colleges, including half the Ivy League. Addams figured in all these lists, and deservedly so, since she probably belonged to more of the accused organizations than any other single person.

The right wing conflation of pacifism and communism was particularly virulent. In May 1922 Gertrude Baer, a respected German educator who had come to address a WILPF conference, was detained as a communist at Ellis Island. Addams and Lillian Wald rushed to Ellis Island to intercede for her, and with great effort were able to convince the authorities that Baer, Secretary of the German branch of WILPF, had no intention of teaching communism. The next year a pamphlet entitled "Peace at Any Price" labeled WILPF's annual conference "the most subversive, certainly the most insidiously and cleverly camouflaged, thoroughly anti-American and un-American" gathering since the war (Alonso 1993, 110). Addams, appealing as always to rationality and decency, repeatedly defended WILPF and described its purpose:

> The League is made up of people who believe that we are not obliged to choose between violence and passive acceptance of unjust conditions for ourselves or others; who believe, on the contrary, that courage, determination, moral power, generous indignation, active good will, can achieve their ends without violence. We believe that experience condemns force as a self-defeating weapon, although men are still so disposed to it as to put it in education, in dealing with crime, in effecting or preventing social changes, and, above all, in carrying out national policies. (JAMSS)

Throughout the 1920s and the 1930s the FBI maintained extensive files on WILPF. It investigated a travel agency that was arranging passage to London for WILPF delegates attending a conference in 1924; it staked out a bookstore in Washington, D.C. run by WILPF members. The Bureau sent agents to local WILPF meetings to spy, and it accepted unsolicited reports from civilian volunteers, which were full of mean-spirited gossip and utterly unverifiable hearsay re-creations of conversations. No allegation was too wild or improbable for inclusion in the files.

The WILPF annual conference in Washington in 1924 drew many delegates from Germany and even Russia. The DAR and the American Legion insisted that the German and Russian women were all communist spies. Addams was so embarrassed by the open hostility of the American press that she apologized to the delegates in her opening remarks. She declared that most Americans were not by nature less tolerant than people in other countries; she blamed the current state of mindless patriotism on the devastating effects of war on human nature. The foreign delegates recognized the inimical atmosphere in which Addams and other American delegates were struggling. After the conference, a German delegate wrote of Addams, "It seemed as if under the chairmanship of Miss Addams, Europe had been given an opportunity to speak freely. The more the foreign delegates realize how unpopular and little understood the Pacifist cause was in the United States, and how difficult it was to swim against the stream, we felt constrained to admire the moral courage of our hostesses" (Sklar et al. 1998, 296).

In 1924 the Daughters of the American Revolution (DAR) denied Addams further membership, declaring her part of a movement bent on the destruction of civilization, government, patriotism, property rights, inheritance, family ties, and Christianity. One Federal agent called her one of the most active radicals in America. In 1926 *Scabbard and Blade*, a promilitary, anticommunist newsletter, listed Addams as a member of 28 organizations, 19 of which it claimed were subversive and/or controlled by communists; they included the American Civil Liberties Union (ACLU), American Peace Society, American Relief for Russian Women and Children, American League to Limit Armaments, American Neutral Conference Committee, American Association for Labor Legislation, WILPF, and many others. *Scabbard and Blade* labeled Addams "the most dangerous woman in America" (JAMSS).

Veterans' groups, medical associations, and even church groups now attacked Hull-House as the center of the evil network. Many of the charges against Hull-House were true: Addams welcomed all sorts of political and social radicals, and frequently offered Hull-House as a safe meeting place for striking workers. One such condemnation, published first in the *Woman Patriot*, was inserted into the *Congressional Record* in 1926 by Senator Thomas Bayard of Delaware: "It is of the utmost significance that practically all the radicalism started among women in the United States centers about Hull-House, Chicago, and the Children's Bureau at Washington, with a dynasty of Hull-House graduates in charge of it since its creation" (*Congressional Record* 1926, 12946).

The DAR continued its attack on Addams in numerous mailings and pamphlets. She was accused of praising the "youth movement," which the DAR called "notoriously a free love institution"; she was condemned as "a very active proponent and member of the National Child Labor Committee" as well as of the notorious ACLU. Among the most damning statements she had made was a demand for "the genuine and unhampered free-dom of the Philippines, Haiti, Nicaragua, and other *colonies and semi-colonies* [emphasis added] (Hamilton 1955, n.p.).

Not all the members of the DAR were comfortable with this campaign. Many thoughtful women were deeply concerned with peace issues as well as with their own revolutionary heritage. A "committee of protest" was organized within the DAR to defend Addams. A letter from the commit-tee to the DAR leadership, published in *The Christian Century*, warned, "The DAR, an organization of high patriotic purpose and select person-nel, is going to have another revolution on its hands if it does not cease to permit itself to be used as the tool of those sinister and reactionary influ-ences which, under the guise of protecting American institutions...are fighting free speech and boosting a big navy" (JAMSS).

Addams replied ringingly to the DAR campaign in 1928, at a meeting of the Pan-Pacific Women's Association in Honolulu. She had been given a questionnaire in advance of the meeting, and she responded candidly to it and took further questions from the audience. "I hope people won't mix up any idea of courtesy in this," she said. "I don't mind heckling. I'm not sensitive, and I believe I've enough English blood in me to rather enjoy it. What you want to do is get your cause and your position before people, and that is the only thing that matters, isn't it?" She pointed out that WILPF asked for no pledge of any sort from members—in truth, almost half the members were Quakers who would not have taken any oath under any circumstances. She vehemently denied the old charges of hav-ing defamed soldiers: "I do not believe if you go through our literature you will find any blame for people who do not agree with us. We certainly do not blame soldiers. We put the responsibility much farther back, to the governments and diplomats." Addams delineated WILPF's philosophy of disarmament as a practical process of three phases: the essential first step was the creation of some method, like the World Court, for the resolution of international disputes. Only when nations could feel reassured of just mediation would they contemplate disarmament: "Nobody will disarm so long as they are afraid. Arms are associated with courage, but really should be associated with fear. It is when we are afraid and suspicious of our neighbors that we want larger armament" ("Questionnaire" 1928, 2–5). The third phase, once political entities were in the process of disarming, would be the gradual elimination of the production of arms and muni-tions.

The image of Addams as a dangerous radical persisted in some quarters almost until her death. As late as 1934 a book entitled *The Red Network* insisted, "Jane Addams has been able to do more probably than any other living woman (as she tells in her own books) to popularize pacifism and to introduce radicalism into colleges, settlements, and respectable circles. The influence of her radical protégées, who consider Hull-House their home center, reaches out all over the world" (Dilling 1934, 51). The statement was probably true in essence, although the intention was scarcely complimentary.

Addams maintained her public poise, but the hostility and hate mail took a terrible toll on her. She confided to a friend that she was having a hard time loving her enemies. Many years later her close friend Alice Hamilton reflected on the effect of all the condemnation and attack on Addams: "she was forced by conviction to work against the stream, to separate herself from the great mass of her fellow countrymen. Nor did she ever fall into the mire of self-pity or take refuge in the comfort of self-righteousness. She simply suffered from the spiritual loneliness which her far-sighted vision imposed on her" (Linn [1935] 2000, xviii).

Chapter 9

ROUNDING OUT A LIFE

The 1920s were a time of profound challenges for Jane Addams. The Great War had left her with a private sense of despair and alienation; she was anguished by the failure of all efforts at mediation and peace making during the war. At home she faced the appalling rise of racism and nativism, and the rightwing condemnations of everything she believed in. Only her work for food relief in Europe gave her a sense of accomplishment. In addition, she was 60 years old in 1920, and her health was deteriorating. Despite her difficulties, Addams maintained her commitment to community activism.

Addams helped found the American Civil Liberties Union in 1920, and served on its national board throughout the 1920s. Concerned as ever with freedom of conscience on an international scale, she was active in the International Committee for Political Prisoners, along with such human rights luminaries as Roger Baldwin, Clarence Darrow, Eugene V. Debs, and W.E.B. DuBois. Addams was one of seven members of the American Commission on Conditions in Ireland, which expressed controversial support for the democratic voices within Ireland's struggle against British occupation. She was a fervent supporter of Sacco and Vanzetti, the Italian anarchists convicted of murder in a politically biased trial in 1920; until their execution in 1927, she was a vocal member of the Sacco-Vanzetti Defense Committee.

Addams remained deeply involved with the tumultuous lives of her impoverished immigrant neighbors in Chicago. Understandably, she took an active interest in crime, crime prevention, and the efficacy of various civic responses to crime; she was committed to the League for the Abolition of Capital Punishment, as well as a strong advocate for reform of the prison parole system. In a devastating speech in Chicago in 1925, she pointed out that the murder rate in the United States was 23 times greater than that in England; the city of Pittsburgh alone had more murders annually than all of England. Clearly, whatever society was doing, whether in prevention or response, was not working. Addams faulted the criminal justice system for too much passion and desire for revenge and for not enough thoughtful analysis. "Reformative justice," she declared, "is getting scant hearing in this fury and turmoil of passionate protest." The entire concept of parole had been abused; it had become "the football of politics" (JAMSS). Clearly, what was needed was a rational, scientific approach, administered by sociological experts, not politicians.

Despite her serious misgivings and the negative analysis the Zurich WILPF conference had given the covenant of the League of Nations, Addams maintained an abiding interest in the organization. She attended the first League meetings in Geneva in 1920, keenly observing both sentiment for disarmament as well as the ominous rise of strident nationalism. She came away from those early meetings strongly convinced that the League, as flawed as it might be, represented the best hope for peace.

The promotion of peace in the world had become the dominant theme of Addams's life. She dedicated more and more of her time and her diminishing energy to WILPF, presiding throughout the 1920s at its congresses in Vienna (1921), The Hague (1922), Washington (1924), Dublin (1926), and Prague (1929). At the third WILPF Congress in Vienna in 1921, Addams received praise and thanks from Friedrich Ebert, first president of the Weimar Republic of Germany, for her efforts at practical reform, internationalism, and relief work. "We can emerge from our current predicament only if the hate generated by years of bloody world war is stopped and the people have the will to work together on rebuilding," he told her. "May these principles, which you have always stood for, finally prevail, and may international peace and social peace crown your work" (Sklar et al. 1998, 259).

WILPF was headquartered in Geneva in the 1920s. Various national branches addressed their own local issues, but the major goal of total disarmament remained a constant. WILPF actively lobbied the League of Nations on many occasions. In 1926 it sent a mission to Haiti to study the problematic United States occupation of that country; the following year a WILPF team went to China and Indo-China to reach out to women's organizations there. WILPF chapters generated a barrage of letters to legislators, reports, classes, summer schools, conferences, marches, and demonstrations. Addams was unquestionably the spiritual symbol of WILPF, although the real quotidian work was done by the dedicated staff in Geneva, ably guided by Emily Greene Balch, German pacifist Vilma Glucklick, and Madeline Doty. When ill health forced Addams to resign as president in 1929, she was promptly elected honorary president for life.

Addams traveled extensively, usually as a peace delegate or a representative of the settlement movement, during those years. She made 12 trips abroad, spending a total of more than seven years outside the United States. Over the previous two decades Addams had fostered an international network of connections with settlements, peace societies, women's colleges, and assorted reform organizations. These contacts now offered her a focus, respect, and welcome that was increasingly scarce in the United States. In January 1923, after the WILPF conference at The Hague, she and Mary Rozet Smith set out on a nine-month trip around the world, spending lengthy visits in India, the Philippines, Japan, Korea, China, and Manchuria. Everywhere she went she was greeted with admiration and tremendous affection; it seemed she was more welcome—and, understandably, perhaps more comfortable—outside her own country than in it.

In 1927 Addams and Emily Greene Balch coauthored a poignant paper entitled "The Hopes We Inherit," in which they summarized the history of pacifism in the West and delineated, once again, the conditions they deemed necessary for the fostering of peace. They acknowledged that their past efforts had been largely unsuccessful but nonetheless, somehow morally necessary: "These futile attempts give at least a certain dignity and traditional background to a contemporaneous endeavor and even suggest an accumulation of moral energy which in the end cannot be withstood" (Addams and Balch 1927, 1). They discussed the biblical prophesy of Isaiah, the nonviolence of Jesus, and St. Augustine's notion of just and unjust war. They examined Mennonite nonresistance during the persecutions of the Reformation and the history of Quaker pacifism.

In addition, Addams and Balch catalogued early ideas for international laws and organizations, ranging from Hugo Grotius's seventeenth-century *On Laws of War and Peace* into the Enlightenment's core faith that Reason would be able to override the passions that lead to hatred and war; they pointed to English Utilitarian philosopher Jeremy Bentham's notions of the greatest good for the greatest number of people, as well as to Immanuel Kant's 1795 paper "Perpetual Peace."

Seen through this internationalist lens, the 1815 Congress of Vienna, which reconfigured Europe after the defeat of Napoleon, offered a sense of possibility and progress; there was at the least discussion of the abolition of slavery, of penal reform and women's rights. In that atmosphere of hope early peace societies were founded in both the United States and England. Later in the nineteenth century the philosophy of peace found eloquent spokesmen in Victor Hugo, Giuseppe Garibaldi, and Leo Tolstoy.

Peace conferences at The Hague in 1899 and 1907 established goals of arbitration and disarmament; the first Hague Court of Conciliation and Arbitration successfully resolved a number of small international disputes before the First World War. After the war, the new League of Nations created the World Court, which also sat in The Hague. Although the United States never officially accepted the protocol of the World Court, an American was always one of the four sitting jurists.

Addams and Balch offered three conditions necessary for nurturing peace: the technological, the capacity for wide and instant communication; the psychological, which through education and communication fosters in people the desire for peace; and the political, the creation of international structures for organized, rational discourse and arbitration. Their hope was that enough of each condition had been met to sustain the possibility of peace. Whatever the challenges and difficulties, it seemed obvious to them that the possibility of peace must be kept alive, that the alternatives were increasingly unthinkable. "It is as practicable to abolish war as it was to abolish the institution of chattel slavery, which also was based on human desires and greed; these are still with us, but slavery has joined cannibalism, human sacrifice and other once sacred human habits, as one of the shameful institutions of the past" (Addams and Balch 1927, 10).

Addams suffered mounting health problems throughout the 1920s; her general health had always been precarious, ranging from frequent illnesses during the 1890s through an appendectomy in 1909 with a slow, complicated recovery, to pneumonia in 1915 and the removal of a kidney the following year. As she aged Addams experienced more frequent illnesses that necessitated lengthier recuperations and left her with diminished energy. The back problems of her youth recurred in chronic backaches, exacerbated by a significant weight gain. She underwent kidney surgery in 1923. Addams suffered a heart attack in 1926 and had to cope with angina thereafter. In 1931 she underwent both lung surgery at Johns Hopkins University Hospital and a mastectomy, which was performed under emergency conditions while she was in Japan. There can be little doubt that her failing health was a factor in Addams's growing sense of displacement, disappointment, and even confusion.

In some profound ways, Jane Addams was still bound by the Victorian morality that had shaped her childhood and youth. She did not drink, disapproved of drinking women, and supported Prohibition. Modest and reserved, she was stunned by the sensuality and the open emphasis on sexuality in the postwar culture of the 1920s; she had always believed in the sublimation of sexual energy as a creative force. Beyond that, she tended to perceive women as vulnerable to sexual exploitation by men, to the extent that she could not fully recognize or appreciate the legitimacy of women's sexuality and desires.

In an era of intense individualism, the attractions of Addams's communal goals faded and she began to seem a little old fashioned, out of step. In the 1920s she no longer topped faddish lists of "most admired" women in America. Addams had never been able to imagine that women's freedom could include the freedom to be selfish, aggressive, and hedonistic. To many young women in the 1920s, Addams's gospel of conscience and responsibility was an intolerable burden: why, they wondered, should women have to be more moral than men? Increasingly, Addams was at odds with her old ally Carrie Chapman Catt. Catt believed women needed to move aggressively into the existing political structure, to hold office and have the opportunity to shape policy. Addams still held that women could reshape the basis of society according to their special mission, their gift for nurture and community activism.

Addams opposed the Equal Rights Amendment, written in 1921 by suffragist Alice Paul to extend unambiguously the Fourteenth Amendment protections to include gender. The amendment was introduced into Congress in 1923, where it was buried in committees and never came to a floor vote; it was proposed in every session thereafter, never even getting out of committee until 1970. (Both Houses of Congress passed the ERA in 1972, but it was three votes short of the required three-quarters' state ratification by the 1982 deadline.) Addams was not alone in her opposition to the ERA. Many social and labor reformers, Florence Kelley and Alice Hamilton among them, feared that the ERA would deny working women the shield of special protective regulations they had spent years constructing. At the other end of the political spectrum, conservatives saw socialist plots in the ERA and feared it as a challenge to existing social structures.

As the attacks on Addams escalated through the 1920s, her old friends and colleagues rallied to her defense. Despite their many differences, in 1927 Carrie Chapman Catt published a blunt refutation of the DAR's charges against Addams in an open letter in *The Woman Patriot*. She de-

clared that Addams did indeed support many social and economic reforms, but only through education and enlightened legislation.

Supporters organized a large testimonial dinner in Chicago in 1927.
President Calvin Coolidge sent his greetings and respect (despite the fact
that Addams had endorsed Robert La Follette for President in 1924). New
York Governor Al Smith was among the public figures who telegraphed
their support and affection that night. William Allen White, a famed crusading journalist who had turned his small-town newspaper, the *Emporia
Gazette,* into a nationally recognized liberal voice, welcomed participants
at the dinner with a moving tribute to Addams:

> If we have nothing to give ourselves but money, and nothing to
> give the world but guns, we are poor indeed.... Jane Addams is
> one who knows that when life moves forward it is following in
> the age-long quest for self-respect.... [Her] vision still lives.
> That dream shall survive our sleep. Miss Addams has followed
> faithfully this great vision through the years. We give her our
> loving gratitude for her life. (Linn [1935] 2000, 372)

Lucy Mead, a leading suffragist and reformer, wrote, "I have known
Jane Addams for over 30 years and have never heard her even under the
strongest provocation utter a bitter or vindictive word." Referring
scathingly to the DAR accusations, Mead wrote, "The whole secret of the
petty and persistent vilification of Miss Addams is that she believes that
war is futile and that the world should stop trying to settle questions of
boundary lines and 'honor' by explosives" (Mead 1927, n.p.). Addams's
long-time fellow pacifist Emily Balch also responded indignantly to the
DAR attacks on Addams: "Is it unpatriotic to want to see the Philippines,
Haiti, Nicaragua, and all other countries *free?* Since when did America
stand for slavery? Cannot equally patriotic people differ as to how early
the Philippines should be given independence?" (Balch 1927, 2).

Pacifists saw a few rays of hope in the darkness of the decade. The
World Disarmament Conference in 1921 resulted in nine treaties on
naval armaments in the Pacific, involving the United States, Britain,
France, Japan, and Italy. The following year these same countries signed
the Five-Power Naval Arms Limitation Treaty; the weakness of these
treaties was always documentation and accountability.

More significant, at least psychologically, was the Kellogg-Briand Pact,
or Pact of Paris, of 1928. The pact grew out of a proposal by French pre-
mier Aristide Briand that France and the United States sign a treaty out-

lawing war between them. Frank Kellogg, then Coolidge's secretary of state, responded that the treaty should be open to other nations. In August 1928, 15 countries signed an agreement that condemned war as an acceptable tool for resolving international disputes; eventually 62 nations signed the Pact agreeing to peaceful discussions before resorting to arms. Even the United States Senate ratified the treaty, by a vote of 85 to 1, although it insisted on an exemption for self-defense that rendered the Pact toothless in America. This was the strongest commitment to peace that major powers had ever made; however, the Pact relied for sanction only on the force of world opinion, and most leaders understood fully how little real power it could wield. Nonetheless, its moral voice was a significant precedent: Justice Robert H. Jackson, chief prosecutor at the Nuremberg Trials in 1945–46, cited Kellogg-Briand as a legal basis for the war crimes trials against prominent Nazis.

Addams drew hope from the Kellogg-Briand Pact. She had always argued that the peace movement would appear logical and inevitable when civilian attitudes prevailed, however gradually, over militarism. In a 1929 speech at the University of Arizona, Addams restated the practicality at the foundation of pacifism: "The great challenge of our time is to offer a satisfactory substitute for war.... Though peace advocates are accused of having their heads in the clouds and their feet well-raised from the earth, they are in reality among the ablest men and women, with every country represented by outstanding leaders" (JAMSS).

As she aged, Addams retreated from the immediacy of daily life at Hull-House; her beloved companion Mary Rozet Smith had created a suite of rooms in her family's Chicago mansion for Addams, and she was more likely to stay there than at Hull-House. Nonetheless, her management style was intensely personal. She was in charge of everything that went on at Hull-House, to a point detrimental to the development of real organization and administrative structures. It was as though she couldn't fully recognize that the demands of Hull-House had grown beyond the capacity of any single person.

The settlement had grown steadily into a complicated, extensive network of buildings, agencies, and programs. Its endowment covered barely one-half the budget, and fundraising was a constant concern. Most of the first generation of prominent benefactors had died, and Addams's reputation was undeniably damaged by an aura of controversy and charges of radicalism that drove away many potential donors. In the ongoing reactionary circus of the 1920s, Addams's income dropped precipitously. From 1905 to 1915, at the height of her prestige, Addams earned an average of

4,000 dollars a year from book sales and lecture fees. Once she was a notorious—and worse, unrepentant—pacifist, many lectures she had been
scheduled to give were cancelled, and sales of her books fell off. Between
1915 and 1930 her annual income was less than $1,500. In five of those
years her income fell below $1,000; she was earning less than many of the
working girls who lived at the Hull-House cooperative boarding houses.
Addams kept detailed financial records; she was painfully aware of this
slide, but she never complained. Despite these very real issues, Addams
insisted on maintaining the independence and integrity of her settlement;
she would never allow Hull-House to join any group charitable drives or
to participate in any Federal programs that might put limitations on policy or practice.

Of necessity, Addams was relentless in her pursuit of funding for Hull-
House. She researched, wooed, cajoled, and badgered potential donors;
she wrote thousands of letters to inspire, exhort, remind, and thank people who could help her. As technology advanced, she used the new tele-
phone to make sure that wealthy people remembered their responsibility
to the poor.

Inevitably, Hull-House aged and changed with Addams. That incom-
parable first generation of activists and dear friends had scattered: Julia
Lathrop and Grace Abbott had gone to Washington, D.C. to important
Federal posts; Alice Hamilton was teaching at Harvard Medical School;
Florence Kelley was running the National Consumers League in New
York City; Ellen Starr, driven by her lifelong spiritual thirst, had con-
verted to Catholicism and entered a convent.

No one at Hull-House had the necessary history or peer relationship
with Addams to permit irreverence or the sort of gentle teasing that had
helped her relax in the old days. There was no one at Hull-House now in a
position to inspire her; rather, in the eyes of many new young residents, she
was relegated to the remote, uncomfortable status of icon. The burgeoning
field of social work now examined social issues through specialized lens
that objectified and pathologized the needy; the social worker addressed
life behaviors with the individual client in a way that could be interpreted
as assigning the client total responsibility for his problems and for fixing
them. What was lost or diminished was the demand for civic, institutional
reforms. The sense of communal responsibility among ethical human beings was further weakened. Ironically, Addams considered herself a sociologist and had never trusted the clinical detachment of social workers.

The year 1929 saw a flurry of celebration in recognition of Hull-House's
40th anniversary. Former residents came from all over the world, as did

hundreds of people who had benefited through the years from the settlement's programs. The prime ministers of both Canada and Great Britain, who had been guests at Hull-House, sent their congratulations and warm regards. John Dewey, a friend since the early days, spoke at the festive banquet of the significance of Hull-House:

> In these days of criticism of democracy as a political institution, Miss Addams has reminded us that democracy is not a form but a way of living together and working together. I doubt if any other one agency can be found which has touched so many people and brought to them a conception of the real meaning of the spirit of the common life. ("Freedom" 1935, 204)

Throughout the late 1920s Addams worked on the sequel to her autobiography, which was published in 1930 as *The Second Twenty Years at Hull-House*. It was a difficult book to write. Ill health and exhaustion plagued her, but beyond that, her spirit and faith in reason had been sorely tested during and after the war, and she could not recapture the joy and ebullience that had made *Twenty Years at Hull-House* so memorable. Addams was openly frustrated and discouraged by the prevalence of bigotry in America. She saw the United States as far behind most European countries in racial attitudes; she predicted that America would be late abolishing racial discrimination just as it had been late abolishing chattel slavery. The book includes chapters on the War, the WILPF congresses, on immigrants and education and anti-immigration legislation and Prohibition, but it lacks the focus and narrative momentum of the earlier book. Addams recognized its failings; when she sent the first chapter off to *The Survey* for possible publication as an article, she admitted that she was disappointed in the chapter and expected her editors to disappointed as well. The drama of lost young Jane finding her path through innovative service had dominated *Twenty Years;* despite Addams's dogged determination to finish the new book, it seemed to her—and to some reviewers— that she had lost confidence in the path she had so proudly chosen 40 years before. In an angry, frightening world with a faster pace of change than she could adjust to comfortably, Addams longed with open nostalgia for the earlier days when both problems and solutions seemed more clear-cut. One reviewer labeled Addams an anachronistic figure, and several others commiserated with her desire to return somehow to the world as it had been before the war.

The artificially booming stock market collapsed on October 29, 1929, triggering an appalling ripple effect and a worldwide depression. The horrors of the Depression, the swelling ranks of the impoverished and dispossessed, demanded some kind of communal and government response. Addams's calls to civic responsibility seemed more relevant than they had in years.

Gradually in the last years of her life, Addams experienced an only partially satisfying rehabilitation as a respected public figure. With religious imagery on the rise, she was increasingly praised as a martyr of selflessness with a special spiritual presence. In the popular press, poems and effusive tributes cast her as a lovable, tired saint who had been sent by God to do his work among the poor. Many articles and children's books about her appeared during these years, churning out the old myths. For the most part the attitude toward Addams was once again sentimental, simplifying her real philosophy and minimizing anything about her that might be disturbing or controversial.

For the moment, Addams was forgiven her pacifism and lack of true patriotism. She began reappearing on lists of most famous, most influential, most recognized women. Addams took all this renewed praise with a grain of salt. When *Good Housekeeping* named her first on its "Twelve Greatest Living Women in America" list, Addams commented tartly, "One of the committee formerly regarded me as a traitor, and I am quite sure that two at least of the others had never heard of me before this 'contest' " (Linn [1935] 2000, 380). Colleges and universities that had shunned her during the war and the tumultuous 1920s began to invite her to speak and to shower her with honorary degrees; she collected awards from Northwestern, University of Chicago, Swarthmore, Rollins, Knox, University of California, and Mt. Holyoke.

In her typical stubborn but genteel manner, Addams managed to say what she believed when she spoke at these colleges. In 1931 her alma mater, Rockford College, chose her as the speaker at a graduation that coincided with her own 50th college reunion. Addams was eloquent on the topic of ethics as a lived process of cooperation and above all mutuality: "May I warn you against doing good to people, and trying to make others good by law? One does good, if at all, *with* people, not *to* people.... Democracy is perhaps not an attainment, but a process..." (Linn [1935] 2000, 387).

Supporters of Addams waged a decade-long campaign to procure the Nobel Peace Prize for her. She was nominated repeatedly between 1920 and 1930; ironically, her uncompromising pacifism and defense of free speech had rendered her too controversial a candidate for the Nobel committee during those years. Finally, in 1931, Addams was considered sufficiently respectable again, and the much coveted prize came to her—but only with an insulting slap: she was forced to share the prize with Nicholas Murray Butler, who as president of Columbia University had supported United States entry into the First World War, worked for the abolition of German language instruction, and fired professors for their opposition to the war. The selection of Butler represented the shabbiest sort of political compromise.

Nonetheless, Addams was elated with the Nobel Peace Prize, although she was recovering from lung surgery and was unable to attend the ceremonies in Oslo. Her share of the prize money was $16,480, which she promptly donated to WILPF. Typically, she instructed the executive committee of WILPF exactly how she wanted the money apportioned: $12,000 was to go into an endowment, with the remainder available for operating expenses; with $500 she repaid herself for a loan she had made to WILPF years before. She urged that WILPF not publicize her gift, because she was wary of giving a false impression of prosperity and financial security.

That same year she was the recipient of Bryn Mawr College's M. Carey Thomas Award, which included a purse of $5,000. In addition, the magazine *Pictorial Review* paid her $5,000 for a photographic essay. All this money Addams simply gave away to the unemployed around Hull-House. When word of her generosity spread, she was flooded with desperate letters from around the entire country, describing overwhelming situations and begging for her help.

In the late 1920s and early 1930s, WILPF continued to work to promote international understanding and disarmament. Numerous parades, protests, and petitions culminated in 1931 a well-organized peace caravan stretching 9,000 miles up and down the country from California to Washington, D.C. At the end, Jane Addams presented President Herbert Hoover with a disarmament petition with more than 500,000 names. The following year a conference on disarmament was held in Geneva. WILPF representatives overwhelmed the delegates with an international petition of over 9 million signatures; there were more than 1.5 million signatures from Great Britain alone.

In 1932 WILPF-USA concentrated its efforts on the rising call for a congressional investigation of the munitions industry and banks and their role in the United States decision to enter the First World War. Senator Gerald Nye of North Dakota introduced a bill calling for such an investigation early in 1934; the bill passed and Nye directed the research of what became the Nye Committee. The work of Nye's committee revealed shockingly high levels of profit from the war, overwhelming propaganda

for the Allies before 1917, and deliberate campaigns to defeat any governmental moves toward regulating the arms industry or reducing Federal
military expenditure. Tragically, these findings were offered in the context
of an isolationism that utterly rejected the kind of international understanding and responsibility that WILPF advocated: the following year the
Senate once again voted down membership in the World Court.

Addams had acquired great respect for Herbert Hoover through her
work with him on famine relief after the First World War; she endorsed
him for president in the election of 1932. When Franklin Roosevelt was
elected, Addams developed great enthusiasm for the programs of the New
Deal, which seemed to embody many of her own principles of social and
communal responsibility. She threw herself into support for Frances
Perkins, Roosevelt's secretary of labor and the first woman cabinet member. Despite her ill health, Addams worked for the Public Works Administration on public housing in Chicago; she was actively involved with the
administration of other New Deal programs in the Chicago area.

During the early 1930s Addams and her colleagues watched the rise of
fascism and repression in Europe and Japan with despair. Addams had always maintained an extensive correspondence with German feminists
and settlement workers. She had a special friendship with Alice Salomon,
a prominent German Jewish social worker. In 1932 Salomon had honored
Addams in *Die Frau,* a major German women's journal: "No living
woman has spoken up for peace more courageously and more bravely and
more effectively...Jane Addams works for peace because war causes not
only hunger and misery, but also because it appears to her as an expression
of hatred and hostility, of the attitude that forms the basis of all social
ills...To her, the interdependency of peoples is the most powerful truth of
our time" (Sklar et al. 1998, 297). The next year, with the election of
Adolf Hitler as chancellor of Germany, Salomon, as a Jew, was effectively
prohibited from further publishing.

Addams wrote urgently about the rise of Nazism, calling upon world
leaders to pay attention. "All that concerns others concerns," she wrote,
"their wrong-doing as well as their sufferings. There must be no self-
righteousness but also no aloofness, no cowardly silence or woolly vague-
ness." She argued that the economic chaos in Germany, the collapse of
the Weimar Republic and the bitterness that nurtured Hitler all grew to a
great extent from the punitive flaws of the Treaty of Versailles:

> Of all the abusive uses of power in the peace treaties, none in a
> way is so spiritually shocking as the war guilt clause, the com-

pelling the German representatives in the name of their people to sign their names to what they believed and were known to believe to be false.... The responsibility for the present state of mind in Germany lies largely with the victors. This is not the place to enumerate the injustices, the bitter hardships of blockade, the humiliation and sense of being condemned from which Germany has suffered. Joined to the exhaustion of the war, the bitterness and confusion of the civil struggles in Germany, the madness of inflation and the ruin of the middle class, the hopelessness of a generation unemployed and without a future—all of these have produced what is apparently a genuine collective psychosis and much of this the "Allied and Associated Powers" are responsible for. (JAMSS)

As usual, Addams refused to accept ethical inconsistencies; while she was scathing in her denunciation of Nazi racial policies, she turned as harsh a light on America's own racial attitudes and history.

It is curious in how many of its phases the Ku Klux Klan resembles the Nazi movement. Its propaganda, its racial and religious intolerance, its lawless beatings and kidnappings, its fiery crosses are curiously similar.... The belief in a caste of color to be upheld at all costs, the economic jealousy of Negro competition, the social and cultural exclusion, the abuses of convict camps, the national disgrace of lynchings and mobmindedness are our direct responsibility.... Even in our attitude toward our Jewish fellow-countrymen we are open to bitter reproach. (JAMSS)

Addams was an increasingly lonely figure as the 1930s progressed. Julia Lathrop and Florence Kelley both died in 1932. Ellen Starr had become an isolated paraplegic, and in March 1934, Addams's beloved companion of 40 years, Mary Rozet Smith, died. Addams herself was seriously ill with bronchitis and bed bound when Smith died of pneumonia; she was unable to attend Smith's funeral. Devastated, Addams went to stay with Alice Hamilton and found some solace in working on a new book, a biography of Julia Lathrop.

In May 1935 WILPF held a congress in Washington, D.C., which Addams attended. She visited the White House and spent quiet time with both Franklin and Eleanor Roosevelt. On May 3 WILPF held a gala dinner in Addams's honor. The roster of appreciative speakers included Harold Ickes, secretary of the interior; Sidney Hillman, leader of the Amalgamated Clothing Workers Union and an old friend; Oswald Garrison Villard, editor of the *Nation;* and Hull-House colleague Alice Hamilton. The National Broadcasting Corporation arranged a technically complex relay that carried coverage of the dinner and speeches from London, Paris, Tokyo, and Moscow as well as Washington. Ickes spoke glowingly of Addams's stalwart defense of civil liberties:

> Serene, unafraid, unheeding of spiteful attacks, she has dared to believe that the Declaration of Independence and the Constitution of the United States were written in good faith and the rights declared in them are rights that are available to the humblest of our citizens. She actually believes that the guarantees of free press, free speech, and free assemblage were not written in a dead language; not devised merely to be copybook models for the improvement of adolescent handwriting, but rights intended to be reserved to the people of the United States and exercised by them. (Douglas 1935, n.p.)

After much more fulsome praise, Addams responded with articulate, humorous modesty. She declared that she knew no such person as had just been so extravagantly described. "You have pointed out how strong have been my convictions on this and that," she mused. "Well, let me tell you that I've seldom been sure that I was dead right. The rightness came after I'd gotten in too far to back out. It had to be right!" (Douglas 1935, n.p.).

One reporter commented, "It is not customary to speak of Jane Addams as a patriot. She is called a humanitarian, a social reformer, an idealist. But is she not one of the great patriots of our national history? What constitutes patriotism? Does one not prove himself a patriot if he cares for the people who live in this nation? Jane Addams is a patriot in that sense" ("A Great Patriot" 1935, 1). The article in the *Washington Post* described her affectionately as "chunky and spunky" and quoted extensively from her speech. "We don't expect to change human nature, we people of peace, but we do hope to change human behavior." That change, she declared, could be achieved only through the slow, careful path of education. "It may not be an inspiring role, but it tests our endurance and our moral enterprise, and we must see that we keep on doing it" (Kihss 1935, n.p.).

Addams was deeply moved by the dinner and she certainly tried to offer her colleagues an energetic façade, but she was utterly exhausted by the hectic schedule she had kept during the WILPF conference. Anna Ickes, wife of the Secretary of the Interior, wrote a detailed description of the dinner to Emily Balch, who was in Switzerland and unable to attend. "Miss Addams was well but frail, and I am glad that this testimonial to her was not postponed" (JAMSS, SCPC).

On May 5, after the WILPF conference, Addams returned to Chicago. Bereft of Mary Rozet Smith, she opted to stay not at Hull-House, but at the home of her oldest supporter, Louise de Koven Bowen. She did go to Hull-House for dinner a few days later, on May 10; it was the last time she would ever see the famous settlement with which she was closely identified. A week later she began to experience abdominal pain severe enough to bring her to Passavant Hospital; exploratory surgery on May 18 revealed advanced, inoperable intestinal cancer. Presented with this dire information when she awoke from the anesthetic, Addams remained calm and cheerful. She had brought a book with her to the hospital, and she joked about finally having a little time to read casually. Friends and family stayed with her constantly; their support kept her spirits strong. On May 20, 1935, she slipped into a coma. The following day, with Alice Hamilton beside her and many nieces, nephews, and friends around her, Jane Addams died. Her death triggered a huge outpouring of grief and praise, most of it genuine, although some of the most fulsome tributes came from the same newspapers that had viciously slandered her in the past.

Addams's body lay in state at Hull-House for two days after her death, in a blaze of bright spring tulips. The hall opened to the public at five in the morning, out of consideration for working people; an estimated 1,500 people each hour came to express their grief, gratitude, and respect. A steady stream of workingmen, lunch boxes in hand, came to kneel and pray beside her coffin. Children kept replenishing the flowers throughout the house. Telegrams of condolence arrived from around the world; it was somehow fitting that Addams's mourners included President Roosevelt, the prime minister of England and the head of state of almost every other country in Europe, as well as hoboes, cooks, waiters and waitresses, the Ladies' Garment Workers Union, and the Bartenders' Union.

It was also fitting that Addams's funeral was held at Hull-House, with music provided by students and teachers of the Hull-House Music School. To many, her death seemed to mark the end of an era of hope and service. Reverend Charles Gilky, a dear friend who officiated at the funeral, quoted her own words: "Progress is not automatic. The world grows better because people wish that it should and take steps to make it better" (JAMSS).

Jane Addams was buried in her family plot in Cedarville. She had chosen her epitaph before her death, to identify what she believed were the
two most important efforts of her long, dedicated life. It reads simply:

Jane Addams
Of
Hull-House
And
The Women's International League
For
Peace and Freedom

CONCLUSION

Much of the world seemed to grieve for Jane Addams. "The entire world mourns her loss," wrote the *Daily Jewish Courier* a few days after her death. "Humanity has lost its best friend" (JAMSS, SCPC). Walter Lippmann, noted author and critic, commented, "She had compassion without condescension. She had pity without retreat into vulgarity. She had infinite sympathy for common things without forgetfulness of those that are uncommon" ("Freedom" 1935, 203). A friend recalled astutely, "She was a woman of marvelous poise. She never seemed to be flustered, never off balance. Even when angry—and she was capable of deep indignation in the presence of evil—she held herself under rigid control" ("Jane Addams" 1935, 252).

Many of the tributes to Addams gushed with the cloying sentimentality that had blurred her image for much of her public life. Others, however, were far more perceptive and sensitive. The *Christian Century* reported bluntly,

> Much nonsense has been written about Miss Addams as "the angel of Hull-House," and an unfortunate amount of it has been repeated in the days immediately following her death ... The very idea requires a complete misconception of Miss Addams's outlook on life. She had no interest in descending to the poverty level. Her interest was in lifting the level all about her to new heights.... Her "theory" of social work, if she had a theory, was always to insist that the fullest possible good be required from the working of existing public and social

agencies, to demand new agencies when the old had been proved inadequate, and to deal with people on the level of their highest potentialities. (JAMSS)

The friends and colleagues who had known her best tried the hardest to debunk the mythology of the saintly Jane Addams. Mary Kingsley Simkhovitch, founder of the New York Settlement Greenwich House and an old friend, insisted, "There was nothing of the super-man about her, separated from the rest of us. Her humanity united us to her. But her naturalness, gentleness, humor and steadfastness made of her a person to be not only loved but revered" ("Freedom" 1935, 209). Alice Hamilton, a member of that astonishing original Hull-House family, commented,

> She had some unusual traits, unusual for a philanthropist and unusual for a woman. For instance, a sort of intellectual integrity that protected her from any touch of sentimentality. She never idealized the poor, the half-baked young radicals, the fanatical reformers who sometimes were pretty difficult, and so she was never painfully disappointed or disillusioned. She never shrank from ugly facts nor refused to listen to damaging evidence. If people were that way, they were, but that did not mean they should be harshly treated. (Hamilton 1935, 2)

Most popular eulogies cast Addams as a paradigm of American virtues, the personification of female benevolence, purity, service, and selflessness. Many commented on her practicality, energy, hard work, and management skills—she came to be honored as a self-made entrepreneur, a quintessentially American wheeler-dealer who had happened to *choose* to work for others. Most writers and speakers distanced themselves from any hint of controversy, usually ignoring the pacifism to which she had dedicated most of her life. Emily Balch had worked intimately with Addams in the women's peace efforts of the First World War and beyond. She utterly rejected the tendency to sanctify and sanitize Addams:

> Someone has said that her prime motive was compassion. I am sure that this is quite wrong... She was full of the love of life— of life as it is, not only as it might be.... I think that her greatness has been veiled by her goodness. Men have a curious tendency to turn those of eminent stature into plaster images. Like her fellow-sufferers in this way, Washington and Lincoln,

she was a statesman. She was a constructive organizer and builder with judgment of extraordinary penetration and sureness, an original intellect incapable of being trammeled by any formula. Her every reaction was intrinsic, original, based on the immediate occasion and never an echo of a previous pronouncement of some one else's or of her own. (JAMSS)

Paul Douglas, a news analyst who had hosted the international broadcast of the WILPF dinner shortly before Addams's death, railed at the hypocrisy of people and organizations that had pilloried Addams in life but lauded her after her death. "Now that she was dead, now that she was out of the way, now that she could no longer defend the weak and helpless, now that she could no longer speak for peace, for kindliness, for justice as between man and man, now it was safe to praise her" (Douglas 1935, n.p.).

Addams was not without unresolved issues in her life. Revisionist historians have charged her with elitism and with proselytizing bourgeois values. Addams was not at all a political elitist, but she was unabashedly convinced that some emotions and goals are more worthy and humane than others. Addams believed that certain kinds of cultural exposure enrich people and foster the more loving, just motives within them. She believed that the values of responsibility, compassion, and tolerance could bring ever greater numbers of people into a widening circle of human rights. While many of Addams's critics in the past accused her of radical socialism and collectivism, her attention was always on individual rights within the context of mutuality, reciprocity, and community; her intense concern for individuals may have contributed to her unwillingness to think in terms of faceless masses, rigid categories, and class conflict. Addams shied away from ideology and dogma, with their labels and restrictions, although much of what she espoused amounted to socialism. Shortly before her death, a niece asked Addams if she was a socialist; she responded, "I am much more nearly one than I used to be" (Haldeman-Julius 1936, 28). Sophonisba Breckenridge, a Hull-House alumna and professor of social service administration at the University of Chicago, wrote after Addams's death, "The characteristic to which I wish to call attention is her unique, in my experience, respect for the freedom of action and of choice of those with whom she was in association" ("Freedom" 1935, 191). Surely this commitment had enabled Addams to welcome war supporters to Hull-House throughout the terrible war years.

As a human being, Jane Addams was not immune to inconsistency and contradiction. She was never fully able to shed all the class assumptions and prejudices implicit in her upbringing. She held on to an idea of the noble poor, who maintained a special kind of simple-hearted wisdom; despite the obvious respect with which she treated her neighbors, she believed that the poor could be encouraged to grow into more refined, upper-class roles. Addams always saw herself as a lady, while the poor mothers and young working women with whom she dealt were just that: women or girls; no matter how democratic her rhetoric, the distinction mattered to her. She appreciated the traditions of the many immigrant cultures with which she dealt, and she urged the first-generation youth to value and maintain their parents' cultures; yet she assumed that American traditions represented a goal for aspiring immigrants. Addams never contradicted the public praise heaped on her for her Christian virtues, but in private she never surrendered her youthful searching skepticism. When her niece asked if she was an agnostic, Addams replied, "I seldom think about it. Intolerance in religion has been responsible for more suffering than any other cause" (Haldeman-Julius 1936, 29). It can be argued that her basic belief in moral evolution implies that not all people are at the same moral stage at any given time—in other words, that some people are morally superior to others. Addams placed her faith in the power of education to awaken the humane conscience, but her own life demonstrated that there were no guarantees of enlightenment.

Addams repeatedly denied any claims of female moral superiority over men, but her theories of Woman's special mission and nurturing responsibility come awfully close to a kind of essentialism. She lived in a raucous inner-city neighborhood and repeatedly confronted sordid behaviors, an enormous range of sexual activity both benign and malignant, and the consequences of assorted human weakness and vice, but her attitudes toward sexuality remained Victorian. The activities she demanded of herself and expected of other women were functional expressions of the generous, sheltering, life-sustaining nature of Woman—the bread giver role in which she had always believed.

Addams died on the eve of the twentieth century's worst cataclysms. For a variety of reasons she sank quickly into a new sort of obscurity. The Spanish Civil War, from 1936 to 1939, provided Hitler and Benito Mussolini with the opportunity to train their troops and to refine their planes and other armaments in the field. The world lurched toward war through the late 1930s, and attempts at compromise, like English prime minister Neville Chamberlain's 1938 meeting with Hitler in Munich, were ill-conceived and horribly short-sighted. The scale of horrors in World War II seemed to discredit pacifism; the Cold War hostilities made a mockery of Addams's hopes for international understanding. American social conservatism after the war and the toxic atmosphere of the McCarthy period echoed the Red Scares and Palmer Raids after the First World War; once again, the generosity and collective responsibility Addams represented were cast into disfavor.

It was not until the 1960s, with the rise of the nuclear disarmament and antiwar movements, that Addams was rediscovered. In the escalating polarization of society, many people could recognize the prescience of Addams's most radical observation: that the most damaging conflict is the intrinsic clash between civil and military cultures, and that there are horrendous long-term costs to society if the military succeeds in dominating the civil. To Addams, the sense of justice depended on mutual understanding and recognition of shared humanity; militaristic nationalism inhibited the development of such communication. In Addams's words, "Mutual understanding sinks deeper and deeper from sight as the bitter waters of war rise higher" (Linn [1935] 2000, 309). Her biographer and nephew, James Linn, argued that she never thought of her efforts in terms of competition, that she could envision peace without victory. He acknowledged that her exhaustive efforts for world peace had been largely fruitless, but he nonetheless saw them as morally essential. "If she failed," he wrote, "she was at least an unforgettable inspiration to others to keep on trying; of all the women of her time, she kept at least the most glowing fire upon the forge" (Linn [1935] 2000, 286).

BIBLIOGRAPHY

WORKS BY JANE ADDAMS

Addams, Jane. 1899. "Democracy or Militarism." Text of an address to The Chicago Liberty Meeting. In *Liberty Tract No. 2*. Chicago: Central Anti-Imperialist League.

———. [1910] 1990. *Twenty Years at Hull-House: with Autobiographical Notes*. Urbana: University of Illinois Press.

———. 1915. "The Revolt Against War." *The Survey*, 17 July, 355–59.

———. 1916a. *The Long Road of Woman's Memory*. New York: Macmillan.

———. 1916b. "Statement of Miss Jane Addams of Chicago, Illinois, representing the Woman's Peace Party." *Hearing before the Committee on Military Affairs*, House of Representatives, 64th Cong., First Sess., 13 June 1916. JAMSS, SCPC.

———. 1920a. "Letter to the Editor." *Chicago Tribune*, 23 February.

———. 1920b. "Nationalism, a Dogma?" *The Survey*, 7 February, 522–26.

———. [1920c?] "Statement on the Situation in Germany." Carbon copy. JAMSS, SCPC.

———. 1922a. "The Aftermath of War." *The Christian Century*, 5 January, 116–18.

———. 1922b. "Peace and Bread: IV: The Witness Borne by Women." *The Survey*, 25 February, 842–69.

———.[1922–1945] 1960. *Peace and Bread in Time of War*. Boston: G.K. Hall & Co.

———. 1928. "Questionnaire: Miss Jane Addams at Mission Memorial Hall, Honolulu, Wednesday Evening, August 22, 1928." Carbon copy. JAMSS, SCPC.

————. 1932. "The Social Deterrent of Our National Self-Righteousness, with Correctives Suggested by the Courageous Life of William Penn." Founders' Day Address, Swarthmore College, 22 October. In *Friends Intelligencer*, 5 November.

————. 1935. *Forty Years at Hull-House*. New York: Macmillan.

————. 1960. *Jane Addams: A Centennial Reader*. New York: Macmillan.

————. 1965. *The Social Thought of Jane Addams*. Indianapolis: Bobbs-Merrill.

Addams, Jane, and Emily Greene Balch. 1927. "The Hopes We Inherit." Unpublished manuscript. JAMSS, SCPC.

Addams, Jane, Emily Greene Balch, and Alice Hamilton. 1915. *Women at The Hague*. New York: Macmillan.

WORKS ABOUT JANE ADDAMS

Alonso, Harriet Hyman. 1993. *Peace as a Women's Issue: A History of the United States Movement for World Peace and Women's Rights*. Syracuse: Syracuse University Press.

Balch, Emily Greene. 1927. "Response to D.A.R. Attacks on Jane Addams and WILPF." Women's International League for Peace and Freedom (WILPF), Swarthmore College Peace Collection (SCPC). Typeset.

Berson, Robin K. 1994. *Marching to a Different Drummer: Unrecognized Heroes of American History*. Westport, Conn.: Greenwood Press.

————. 1999. *Young Heroes in World History*. Westport, Conn.: Greenwood Press.

Chamberlain, Mary. 1915. "The Women at the Hague." *The Survey*, 5 June, 219–31.

Chambers, John Whiteclay II, ed. 1991. *The Eagle and the Dove: The American Peace Movement and United States Foreign Policy 1900–1922*. Syracuse Studies in Peace and Conflict Resolution. Syracuse: Syracuse University Press.

Curti, Merle. 1961. "Jane Addams on Human Nature." *Journal of the History of Ideas* 22 (2): 240–53.

Davis, Allen F. 1973. *American Heroine: The Life and Legend of Jane Addams*. New York: Oxford University Press.

Davis, Allen F., and Mary Lynn McCree, eds. 1969. *Eighty Years at Hull-House*. Chicago: Quadrangle Books.

De Benedetti, Charles, ed. 1986. *Peace Heroes in Twentieth Century America*. Bloomington: Indiana University Press.

Degen, Marie Louise. [1939] 1972. *A History of the Woman's Peace Party*. New York: Garland Press.

"Deplores Pacifist List." 1919. *New York Times*, 27 January. Incomplete clipping, JAMSS, SCPC.

Detzer, Dorothy. 1938. "Memories of Jane Addams." *Fellowship* (September).

Diliberto, Gioia. 1999. *A Useful Woman: The Early Life of Jane Addams*. New York: Scribners.

Dilly, Elizabeth. 1934. *The Red Network*. Chicago. Milwaukee: C.N. Caspar.

Douglas, Paul H. 1935. Radio address, 29 May. JAMSS, SCPC.

Ehrenreich, Barbara, and Deirdre English. 1978. *For Her Own Good: 150 Years of Experts' Advice to Women*. New York: Doubleday.

Ellen Gates Starr Papers. Sophia Smith Collection, Smith College, Northampton, MA.

Elshtain, Jean Bethke. 2002. *Jane Addams and the Dream of American Democracy: A Life*. Cambridge, Mass.: Basic Books.

Farrell, John C. 1967. *Beloved Lady: A History of Jane Addams' Ideas on Reform and Peace*. Baltimore: Johns Hopkins Press.

Fischer, Marilyn. 2004. *On Addams*. Wadsworth Philosophers Series. Australia, United States: Thomson/Wadsworth.

Foner, Philip S. 1982. *Women and the American Labor Movement: From the First Trade Unions to the Present*. New York: The Free Press.

Foster, Catherine. 1989. *Women for All Seasons: The Story of the Women's International League for Peace and Freedom*. Athens: University of Georgia Press.

"Freedom, Fellowship, and Character in Religion." 1935. *Unity* 115, no. 10 (July).

Gilman, Catheryne Cook. 1948. "Jane Addams, the Universal." Paper read at Women's International League for Peace and Freedom, 20 February, Minneapolis, Minnesota. JAMSS, SCPC.

"A Great Patriot." 1935. *The American Observer* 4, no. 35 (May).

Haldeman-Julius, Marcet. 1936. *Jane Addams as I Knew Her*. Reviewer's Library no. 7. Girard, Kans.: Haldeman-Julius Publications.

Hamilton, Alice. 1955. "Jane Addams of Hull-House and the WILPF." *The Round Table* 19, no. 6 (June).

Hansen, Jonathan M. 1997. "Fighting Words: The Transnational Patriotism of Eugene V. Debs, Jane Addams, and W.E.B. DuBois." Ph.D. diss., Boston University.

Hapgood, Norman, ed. 1927. *Professional Patriots: An Expposure of the Personalities, Methods, and Objectives Involved in the Organized Effort to Exploit Patriotic Impulses in These United States During and After the Late War*. New York: Albert and Charles Boni.

"Jane Addams." 1935. *Christian Century*, 5 June, 251–55.

Jane Addams Manuscripts, Swarthmore College Peace Collection, Swarthmore, Pennsylvania.

Jane Addams *Papers on Microfilm*. 1985. Mary Lynn McCree Bryan (ed.). Ann Arbor, MI: University Microfilms International.

Kennedy, David M. 1980. *Over Here: The First World War and American Society.* Oxford: Oxford University Press.

Kihss, Peter. 1935. "Jane Addams' Plea for Peace." *Washington Post,* 3 May. JAMSS, SCPC.

Kuhlman, Erika A. 1997. *Petticoats and White Feathers: Gender Conformity, Race, the Progressive Peace Movement, and the Debate Over War, 1895–1919.* Westport, Conn.: Greenwood Press.

Lasch, Christopher. 1965. *The New Radicalism in America, 1889–1963: The Intellectual as a Social Type.* New York: W.W. Norton.

Levine, Daniel. 1964. *Varieties of Reform Thought.* Madison: The State Historical Society of Wisconsin.

Linn, James Weber. [1935] 2000. *Jane Addams: A Biography.* Urbana: University of Illinois Press (Linn was Addams's nephew, knew her intimately, had access to all her papers, and worked directly with her on this biography.)

"Liquor and Bayonet Charges." *Evening Post (New York),* 14 October. JAMSS, SCPC.

Lovett, Robert Morss. 1946. "Jane Addams and the W.I.L.P.F." Address by Robert Morss Lovett at the tea commemorating the birthday of Jane Addams, 26 October, at Hull-House, Chicago. JAMSS, SCPC.

Lynd, Staughton, ed. 1966. *Nonviolence in America: A Documentary History.* Indianapolis: Bobbs-Merrill.

Mead, Lucia Ames. 1927. "Defends Jane Addams" (Letter to the Editor). *The Transcript,* 20 June.

Miller, Randall M., and Paul A. Cimbala, eds. 1996. *American Reform and Reformers: A Biographical Dictionary.* Westport, Conn.: Greenwood Press.

Millis, Walter. 1935. *The Road to War: America 1914–1917.* Boston: Houghton Mifflin.

Murphy, Paul L. 1979. *World War I and the Origin of Civil Liberties in the United States.* New York: W.W. Norton.

Phillips, J.O.C. 1974. "The Education of Jane Addams." *History of Education Quarterly* 14, no. 1 (Spring): 49–67.

Reed, Christopher Robert. 1997. *The Chicago NAACP and the Rise of Black Professional Leadership, 1910–1966.* Bloomington: Indiana University Press.

Report of the International Congress of Women, 12–17 May 1919, Zurich. 1920. Geneva.

Schott, Linda. 1993. "Jane Addams and William James on Alternatives to War." *Journal of the History of Ideas* 54, no. 2 (April): 241–54.

Sklar, Kathryn Kish. 1990. "Hull House in the 1890s: A Community of Women Reformers." In.*Unequal Sisters: A Multicultural Reader in United States Women's History,* edited by Ellen Carol Dubois and Vicki L. Ruiz. New York: Routledge.

Sklar, Kathryn Kish, Anja Schuler, and Susan Strasser, eds. 1998. *Social Justice Feminists in the United States and Germany: A Dialogue in Documents, 1885–1933*. Ithaca: Cornell University Press.

Stebner, Eleanor J. 1997. *The Women of Hull House: A Study in Spirituality, Vocation, and Friendship*. Albany: State University of New York Press.

"Stevenson's 'Disloyal' List Fights Back and Asserts He Lies." 1919. *The Call* 26 January.

Swarthmore College Peace Collection. Swarthmore, PA.

Villard, Oswald Garrison. 1935. "Issues and a Woman: Jane Addams and Her League." *The Nation*, 29 May, 619.

Woman's Peace Party Papers, SCPC.

Women's International League for Peace and Freedom Papers, SCPC.

Young, Rose, ed. 1935. *Why Wars Must Cease*. New York: Macmillan.

INTERNET SOURCES

http://www.rockford.edu/inaugural/janeaddams.htm (JA Center for Civic Engagement).

http://www.rockford.edu/about/janeaddams.aspx (Rockford College).

http://www.swarthmore.edu/library/peace/DG001-025/DG001Jaddams/ cklist.html (Jane Addams Collections Checklist, Swarthmore College Peace Collection).

http://www.uic.edu/depts/lib/specialcoll/services.rjd/jamc.shtml (Janes Addams Memorial Collection, University of Illinois at Chicago).

http://www.uic.edu/jaddams/hull/hull_house.html (Hull House Museum).

INDEX

About the Author

ROBIN K. BERSON is an independent scholar and director of the Upper School Library, Riverdale Country School, Bronx, New York.